Nothing For Tears

Lali Horstmann came from a distinguished German banking family, the van Schwabachs. Her husband Freddy Horstmann was a diplomat and art collector, the only son of the owner of a Frankfurt newspaper, the General Anzeiger. Freddy Horstmann resigned from the Diplomatic Service when Hitler came to power. Lali Horstmann left Berlin in 1949, and lived mostly in London and New York. She died in 1954.

NOTHING FOR TEARS

Lali Horstmann

With an introduction by
Harold Nicolson

PHOENIX
PRESS

5 UPPER SAINT MARTIN'S LANE
LONDON
WC2H 9EA

3 1257 01394 2304

A PHOENIX PRESS PAPERBACK

First published in Great Britain
By Weidenfeld & Nicolson in 1953
This paperback edition published in 2000
by Phoenix Press
a division of The Orion Publishing Group Ltd,
Orion House, 5 Upper St Martin's Lane,
London WC2H 9EA

Printed and bound in Great Britain by
Butler & Tanner Ltd, Frome and London

ISBN 1 84212 212 6

" Nothing is here for tears, nothing to wail
Or knock the breast; no weakness, no contempt,
Dispraise or blame; nothing but well and fair
And what may quiet us in a death so noble."

—SAMSON AGONISTES.

Introduction

WHAT HAPPENS in civilized communities when suddenly, between a sunset and a dawn, the bulwarks of security are shattered and the barbarians break in? Often, when visiting a ruined Roman villa on some lazy summer afternoon, have I pictured to myself the night of horror, when the woods became alive with shouts and torches, and a pool of blood slid slowly across the tessellated pavement, obscuring the figure of Europa, seated plump and flattered astride her bull. As the sky began to lighten in the east, the burning beams would fall hissing one by one among the gold-fish in the fountain, and when the roof collapsed the hills would echo with the clatter of falling tiles and the yews and beech-trees would flicker, strangely green, in the last blaze of holocaust. For a little while a wounded dog, escaped into the coppice, would howl in agony. Thereafter would descend the silence of four hundred years.

More pertinently, sometimes, I ask myself what would occur if next October Russian parachutists descended from the sky upon my own calm patch of Kent and if the news seeped through from London that all organized resistance was at an end. I suppose that I should myself be quickly liquidated, or bundled into the farm lorry (together with the vicar, the schoolmaster and a few local koulaks) and driven, on the wrong side of the road, to the concentration camp at Biggin Hill. But what would happen to those left behind? The books, the pictures and the china would, I suppose, be quickly defaced, slashed and broken as intolerable evidence of capitalist decadence. Much time would be spent by the marauders in searching for hidden treasure or stores of non-existing wine. The garden hedges and the rose-trees would be hacked down in irritation; the donkey, the swan and the turtle doves would all be killed; I doubt whether even the Muscovy ducks would be acclaimed as comrades. A litter of clothes, curtains, notepaper and old copies of the Burlington Magazine would be scattered among the irises, and above it all the tower clock would continue to strike the hours, as if everything were just the same as it had been ten days ago.

What interests me particularly is to speculate regarding the treatment that would be accorded to, and the behaviour that would be adopted by, all those of the village who have lived with us and among us for more than twenty years. A Kommandatura of sorts would, I suppose, be set up in the village hall, and men and women would queue up to be registered and screened. Would they be frightened, angry, or just amused? Would they be loyal to each other, or would the secret animosities of rural life tempt a few mean souls to treachery and denunciation? Would the shortage of food and fuel obliterate all other anxieties, all acquired customs, and reduce these men and women to the status of animals, creeping fox-like in the night? Could they control themselves when they heard the screams of their wives and mothers being raped by Tartars? Or would all this sudden savagery become infectious and lead them to dance drunkenly, arrayed in the vicar's surplices, around the bonfires on the green?

Probably it would all happen much as it happened in the story that is here presented. A retired diplomatist of taste and means was living with his wife in an elegant manor house in the home counties. All his life he had been a collector of works of art and had remained an optimistic, obstinate and self-indulgent man. It would have been possible for him, when the Russian armies approached, to escape with his wife to the western zone. He refused to credit the stories told by the refugees who had fled before the oncoming barbarians. Being an intellectual and a man of the world, he believed that things were never as bad as imagined, or related, by less cultivated minds. Even the most outrageous Tartar could be tamed by a little dexterity, a show of confidence, a few well placed bribes. Above all he felt a deep loyalty to his own possessions, to those lovely objects of crystal, porcelain and enamel that he had collected all his life. It would be cowardly to forsake them. And thus, when the barbarians streamed into his village, he sought to ignore their existence, amusing himself by rearranging the china upon his chimney-piece, designing a new garden pavilion, or estimating the effect of a bunch of forsythia in a dark blue vase. It was only gradually that the full horror descended on the manor house. There was nothing sudden about the process; it came slowly and increased in intensity night by night. At first they said to each other: "Well, after all it is not quite so awful as we anticipated." Within a week they were saying: "Nothing, nothing, that we ever imagined could be as terrible as this." But by then it was too late.

It is not my business to anticipate Frau Horstmann's narrative. It is my business to assure the reader that every word of this book is true. This is what actually happened to people such as we are, living in Germany at the time of the Russian invasion. It is indeed valuable to possess such a document, written by a woman of rare integrity and gifts.

(2)

When, between the years 1926 and 1929, I served in Berlin as Counsellor of the British Embassy, Freddy Horstmann was head of the English department of the German Foreign Office. It was with him that I had to conduct such day-to-day negotiations as were not of sufficient importance to be dealt with directly between my Ambassador and the Minister for Foreign Affairs. I saw him frequently, and at an early stage of our acquaintance he asked me to his house and introduced me to his wife, the writer of this book.

Since the signature of the Locarno Treaties in 1925, almost normal relations had been re-established between Germany and her former enemies. The period of inflation had by then been succeeded by a surge of seeming prosperity and by a fevered display of intellectual and artistic invention. Berlin society had not, however, recovered from the shock of defeat or the liquidation of the old imperial hierarchy. The great houses were closed; the Herrenklub had retired into sullen seclusion; the former aristocracy and the members of the military élite were resolved—and it was to their credit—not to entertain foreigners, or to accept their hospitality, so long as the allied armies remained in occupation of German soil. Our social contacts were thus confined to the dreary round of diplomatic intercourse, from which we escaped gladly into the vivid and licentious Bohemia that bubbled and scintillated in the western quarter of Berlin.

From time to time would occur government dinners of slow solemnity. I would sometimes be asked to luncheon at the villa occupied by Herr Stresemann in the garden of the Wilhelmstrasse and I acquired a deep admiration for the versatility of that ill-used statesman, a real affection for Frau Stresemann and her sons. Frau von Schubert, the wife of the permanent head of the German Foreign Office, would regularly invite the members of foreign missions and we were as impressed by the dignity of her bearing as we were by the vintages that her husband would supply from his estate at Treves. Such occasions were for me clouded by my distaste for all forms of official entertainment. Only in the house of Freddy and Lali Horstmann was I able to divest myself of the cope of diplomatic convention and to find the ease that comes from association with people who, whatever their nationality, share the same thoughts and feelings and are interested in the same sort of things.

At that date Freddy Horstmann enjoyed a considerable private fortune, derived from the *General Anzeiger*, a newspaper

owned by his family in Frankfurt. He and his wife lived in a
large house in the Park Lane of Berlin, the Tiergartenstrasse.
The rooms on the ground floor looked out upon the garden
and were darkened by curtains, tapestries and heavy Turkish
rugs. Chandeliers of silver and crystal hung from the ceiling;
his snuff-boxes were displayed in cases against the walls; there
were china figures upon the chimney-piece and baroque mirrors
shimmered in the recesses of the room. In the evening there
would be candles in sconces and fine candelabra upon the
table-cloth, in the centre of which there was always a different
Meissen bowl, or a delicate glass goblet of the early eighteenth
century. He had considerable knowledge of the work of the
German and Austrian silversmiths and would show us fine
examples of the best period, handling them with heavy but
loving fingers, and talking to us about Altdorfer or Zan. The
food was excellent, the guests chosen for their charm rather
than for their official position, the discourse varied, and the
physical and intellectual comfort carefully contrived. One had
the impression that he planned his parties with amused
ingenuity, combining disparities as cleverly as he would combine unusual flowers in a bowl. He was always the artist, intent
upon proportions, contrasts and values. The effect might have
been one of rather cumbrous artificiality, had not Lali Horstmann been there to add the touch of simplicity, gentleness and
grace.

(3)

After I had left Berlin, Freddy Horstmann was appointed
German Minister to Belgium and thereafter to Portugal. I
never saw Lali Horstmann in her ambassadorial capacity, but
I am sure that she performed her functions with the same
naturalness as she performs every function. Patient and amused,
she coped with Freddy's egoism, smiling quietly when he became
querulous, selflessly providing him with the comforts and
pleasures that he demanded as his natural right. During those

years I would meet her occasionally when she was on leave, in London or Paris, in Austria or Venice. Our friendship, although often interrupted, remained constant; always we would start again exactly where we had last left off. Even after six years of war, even after the atrocious experiences narrated in this story, even among the charred ruins of what had once been Berlin, I found her still the same calm, uncomplaining, dignified friend that I had always known. She was too interested in the experiences of the mind, too quietly confident of the affection of those she loved, to worry about the loss of wealth or possessions. Hers was no simulated resignation: the material had for her been always immaterial: all that she wanted was to recover sufficient health to start life over again.

She was much younger than her husband. Her father, Herr von Schwabach, came of a distinguished banking family and was a man of culture and repute. He had been a friend of the Emperor William II, with whom he differed in regarding as provocative the propaganda of the Flottenverein and the obstinacy of Admiral von Tirpitz in creating a High Seas Fleet and thereby arousing the fears, and eventually the animosity, of Great Britain. For many years Herr von Schwabach served in the capacity of honorary British Consul-General in Berlin: he had been accorded by Queen Victoria the rare honour of a K.C.M.G.

Lali was born cosmopolitan, speaking French and English as easily as she spoke her native tongue. To her an understanding of art, music and literature was no pretentious acquisition: it had come to her, almost in childhood, as naturally as her pets, her dolls, her governesses, her affections and her taste. She never strove for effect; she achieved it without effort and by the calm of her reserve.

When Hitler came to power, Freddy Horstmann, not liking such company, resigned from the Diplomatic Service. He was regarded with suspicion by the Nazi authorities, who in revenge commandeered the newspaper that he owned. The house in the

Tiergartenstrasse was disposed of and a small ground-floor flat taken in the Stein-Platz. This flat, by some miracle, survived the final bombardment almost unscathed; it was here that Lali Horstmann took refuge when eventually she escaped from the Russian zone. It was here that I found her again in 1947, recovering slowly from her ordeal and feeling safe at last in the protection of her many British and American friends.

After their retirement from the Diplomatic Service, the Horstmanns had lived mainly at Kerzendorf, a property that she had inherited from her parents, some fifteen miles to the east of Berlin. There was a small park, with avenues and statues, a garden, and an eighteenth-century house of elegance and charm. This house was destroyed one night by allied bombers and only a black shell remained. The Horstmanns then moved into the agent's little house in the park, to which they transferred such of the panelling and tapestries as they had been able to rescue from the fire or to bring from Berlin. It contained a large living-room in white and gold in which Freddy was able to dispose of his varied collections and to recreate some reflection at least of a lavish collector's past. It was in this small house that occurred the events related in this story.

Then the Russians came, and one spring night in 1946 the Secret Police arrived and took Freddy away with them into the dark. It was two and a half years before Lali, in spite of her anguished efforts, learnt, almost by chance, that he had died of starvation in a Russian concentration camp, only a few miles from his home.

In reading this story, narrated with such excellent restraint, the reader may derive an impression of Lali Horstmann as a woman of powerful physique, able to lift huge wardrobes, and to cow cossacks by the squareness of her jaw. This would be an incorrect impression. She is in fact a fragile, Marie Laurençin, little figure, with enormous eyes. Which enhances her audacity and our esteem.

HAROLD NICOLSON

Chapter I

BEHIND ME is the destruction and dispersion of houses I have lived in or known and beings I have loved. Palpable stone and mortar, which, we believed, was certain to outlive our own existence, proved to be made of the stuff of which we build our dreams. Yet, although in looking back I see catastrophes and losses as milestones marking the last years, the emphasis is not on them, nor on the anguish they caused. It is not the impression of fear that remains from hours of danger, but of a branch white with snow against a blue sky, or a memory of the ominous beauty of silver planes glittering in the sun. A word of friendship or a letter brought a warm relief from the horrors of war, for they could be woven into the continuity of personal consciousness that flows through good times and bad, as a river flows with the same force through barren and fertile country alike. Events had an importance through their historical and political consequences, yet they created but a frame to enclose life's intimate reality as it was felt by each separate human being. Accidents killed, but death itself remained the same eternal experience. Happiness could remain undisturbed under a bombardment or amidst material difficulties, while supreme misery was possible in days of outward calm.

In learning about the French Revolution, we are surprised to discover that balls were held and theatres filled during the cruellest period of the terror, that men and women doomed to die had even danced in prison. It is foolish to assume that people are capable of brooding ceaselessly on their own terrible fate, or can be endlessly absorbed in compassion for the misfortunes of others. One forgets that the necessity for food, for protection against heat and cold, for pleasure as a diversion from tension, are part of the eternal rhythm of day and night. Each moment has its specific demand, and those involved in tragedy realize their fate less than people watching from afar.

On the day before I left Berlin for ever, a friend took me through the town to let me say a last farewell to places where I had spent my life. We left the busy British and American sectors for streets formerly animated by crowds and cars, where now the only sound was made by an occasional piece of broken wall detaching itself to fall to earth in a cloud of dust. I stood for a long while before the charred façade of my parents' house, moved by seeing remnants of the familiar rooms between the crumbling stones. As the cold shadow of the staring ruins half covered me, I was overcome by the temptation to give up striving to live, to give in to death as to an overwhelming desire for sleep. I fought like a drowning man to recapture the memory of the dead whose wish I knew it was that their own existence should survive through my person, and whose conceptions and beliefs were in contrast to the static scene that was dangerously claiming me. After long hesitation, I made the effort. I turned my back on the inanimate house and crossed the street to walk on in the sun.

As I looked at the empty houses I thought of people who had been forced to abandon them. Their various destinies came to my mind, and brought back the many anecdotes, gay and sad, private and political, that I knew about them. I longed to be an Oriental story-teller standing at a street corner, attracting listeners with his tales of incidents that stirred him, and arousing laughter and tears with the kaleidoscope of his own memories.

A large stone gate, the Brandenburger Tor, admitted us into the non-European world of the Russian sector. The few passers-by were mostly soldiers with Asiatic faces, striding about with a broad, confident gait.

The only house left standing in the large square, the Pariser Platz, where every building had historical associations, though

2

none possessed architectural beauty, was the Hotel Adlon. It had been the centre of Berlin life for many years. Its owner, old Mr. Adlon, had been killed by a drunken soldier at the end of the war, and now the hotel was used only by a few business men from the Eastern Zone. On the opposite side of the square was the façade of the French Embassy and the remains of what had been the famous 'Herren-Club', whose members were reactionary country gentlemen. Some of them like General Schleicher, who was assassinated by Hitler, or Franz von Papen, had exercised a considerable political influence.

Next door another vestige of the past was the house of Princess Radziwill, who had played a great role in the social and political life of Berlin in a former generation. She came from the French family of the Counts of Castellane, while her husband, though a Pole, was a Russian subject, since Poland had ceased to exist after its partition. He had been Adjutant to the Czar Alexander II, who had assigned him as an act of special courtesy to serve the first German Emperor, William I, his cousin, in the same capacity at the court of Berlin. Relations between countries were then so close, that Prince Radziwill, though he never surrendered his Russian nationality, remained in this confidential position until the end of his life. His wife, who lived until 1915, was one of the last of a line of great ladies who gained an international position through the offices held by various members of her family at the Courts of Russia, Germany and Austria and through her connections with France. Unfortunately, the Emperor Wilhelm II, although personally devoted to her for his grandfather's sake, did not listen to her wise advice, based though it was on sound information.

We went through the Foreign Office, once humming with activity, on to my grandparents' house, where I paid my last respects as if to their tomb, and then walked down the streets where dignified buildings, that once had been important banks, lay silently decaying. Their grey dilapidation was plainly denied any future. It contrasted strangely with the whitewashed walls

3

of the 'House of Culture', the centre of Russian propaganda, that stood out with a sharp brilliance amidst its sordid surroundings, its interior decorated with the impersonal luxury of a brand new hotel, with hangings and carpets of bright red, and gilt furniture ornamenting the foyer, the large lecture-rooms and the banqueting halls. In the restaurant excellent food, then a rarity in Berlin, and vodka were served. The rooms were hung with propaganda posters designed to influence the minds of students, intellectuals and workers, by an arbitrary juxtaposition of photographs proving the 'lack of humanity' and 'social irresponsibility' of Western democracy. One, showing a child dying of tuberculosis in a miserable room, was placed next to a picture, with the caption 'A dog manicure', that depicted a woman trimming the nails of a Pekinese. Another of Princess Elizabeth cutting her large wedding cake was contrasted with a photograph of Indians begging for food and worn to skeletons by starvation.

I visited the Russian bookshop in the Potsdamer Platz, where we found interesting records of modern music, but the books consisted solely of Soviet propaganda, the doctrinaire writings of Karl Marx, Lenin and Stalin, obtainable in all languages. The works of their great classical writers, Dostoievsky, Gogol and Tolstoy, were entirely absent. The only volume of Turgeniev available was one bitterly critical of the former social order.

On the way home we walked through what had been a park lying in the middle of the city that had once been laid out in lawns covered with crocus and tulips and surrounded by flowering shrubs. They had now vanished, together with the three-hundred-year-old trees that had been cut down and used for fuel by the population in the cold winter of 1946–47. A small, sad desert had taken the place of the graceful garden. Nothing was recognizable to recall the scene where for centuries children had played, and lovers had met in secluded places now open to every wind, and politicians had discussed their secret plans, while riders trotted by on glossy horses. In winter there had been skating on the lake, named after Jean Jacques Rousseau, and whispering couples had walked around its sheltered paths in the afternoon dusk, observed with curiosity by little girls accompanied by their governess. Trees, grass, flowers, had melted like the ice on the lake. Only the statues remained as witnesses of their vanished existence and stood out incongruously from a now flat field. The last Emperor had erected a long double row of figures in honour of his family, the Hohenzollern, in a stark white marble that gave them the appearance of wax works. He had called it 'Alley of Victory', a name that from the beginning must have seemed a challenge to the Gods. The statues were glaringly visible from afar, although their stone hands, swords and legs were scattered on the ground like enormous broken dolls, with a huge decapitated head of Bismarck lying in the middle of the alley, face upward, its large vacant eyes opened to the sky above. The riot of marble was surrounded by tiny depressing plots in which people had tried in vain to grow cabbage and potatoes in the sandy soil, in a helpless fight against chaos more distressing than the romantic grandeur of abandoned buildings.

Looking back on that last day in my native city, my thoughts revert to the final months of the war, to the dissolution of a country that took place before my eyes, and to the first period of the occupation of Germany as I witnessed it. Now at a distance from the ravaged soil of Europe, I still have the diary which I kept day by day, and which I have used as notes in writing of these last days.

Chapter II

AT THE end of 1944, in the last months of the interminable war, my husband and I were staying with his sister, Countess Elly Donna, at her house in Buckow, sixty miles east of Berlin, where we had moved some months before, after my childhood home in the country had been demolished by bombs. In the 1870's my grandfather, who was a banker, had bought the small estate of Kerzendorf with its eighteenth-century house. It was only fifteen miles from his town-house and office in the centre of Berlin, and when he had installed his wife and three sons in the country at the beginning of May, it was easy for him to join them every evening and spend his week-ends there, always surrounded by a great number of guests—politicians, diplomats, businessmen and friends of every description—until in October the house was closed and the furniture put to sleep under chintz covers. When my parents married, they built a bungalow in the park for themselves. On my grandfather's death, they took over the larger house and my father, who in turn became head of the bank, went to and fro from town to country. He and my mother were even more hospitable, as by then motor-cars had reduced the distance from the city. I was deeply attached to Kerzendorf by innumerable childhood memories and by my long intimacy with the people and countryside. It was with regret that I returned every autumn to the brilliant round of social life in the capital.

After 1933, when my husband resigned from the diplomatic service, his conscience forbidding him to serve under National-Socialism, I visited my parents even more often as a rest from the city existence I was leading in our apartment in Berlin.

6

Freddy, my husband, was a strong, bulky man twenty years my senior, whom I had married very young. He was the only adored son—with two sisters—of the owner of a newspaper in Frankfurt-am-Main.

He was an ambitious youth, eager for position and honours, in love with life, with women, with beauty in any form. He had been strongly influenced by the Patrician culture of Frankfurt, which had its roots in the time when the Emperors of the Holy Roman Empire were crowned there, and had flourished as a highly developed form of civilization long before the Prussian kings had made their country powerful. He had been brought up to admire the houses of the Bethmanns, Grunelius, Rothschilds and others. From childhood onwards he had before him the example of collectors who vied with one another in buying objects at the antique shops, where some of them would meet around noon to discuss their discoveries and temptations. My husband's preoccupation with collecting was matched by keeping his house as perfectly as possible. As this had been one of his delights before our marriage, during the long time he lived in Paris and in the four years he was attached to the Embassy at Washington, he took over all practical questions of daily existence with the indefatigable zest he put into everything. He steered all worries away from me, but although my health was not strong, I shared his insatiable curiosity for people and the amusement he derived from entertaining them. He had guests at every meal unless we were ourselves invited out. He was much older than myself, yet his unflagging vitality far exceeded mine, and carried me along somewhat baffled and overwhelmed: for he lived in a whirl of activity, plans, appointments, all undertaken with an imagination so lively, that the twenty-four hours of the day were insufficient. Even after a heart attack, the result of an exciting tennis match in a burning sun, when he had to be careful not to exert himself, he gave up nothing of what was essential to him.

He was obstinate, he was selfish, he was spoiled—his father,

7

his life and myself had seen to that—but he was generous, warm-hearted and lovable, and his instinctive knowledge of human nature made him aware of people's passions and feelings. He had fitted his intelligence and the intensity of his nature to the rules of the Edwardian world during the years of his formation. Would he, an individualist of the purest dye, to the point of eccentricity, find his way through the wilderness of events now opening before us?

Freddy had become as much attached to Kerzendorf as I was, and when my mother died in 1942, leaving it to us with the many things it contained, we decided to live there, only keeping our little apartment in Berlin as a *pied-à-terre*. Some of the collector's pieces we took to a bank in the city, but most of them remained in the house in Kerzendorf, except for some that were stacked in a shed, waiting to be unpacked when peace should return one day.

Kerzendorf lay ten miles away from the Daimler aircraft works, at what we had thought to be a safe distance. Many of our friends had placed a wide variety of objects such as cameras, clothes, Picasso drawings and silver, in our care, miscalculating the chances of war. For in order to save the factory, the German authorities had suspended clusters of glowing balloons, 'Christmas Trees' people called them, over innocent villages, which were then attacked by Allied pilots who mistook them for their targets. The placing of these decoys had the result that the Daimler plant, built three-quarters of the way underground with the exposed parts carefully camouflaged in dark olive-green paint, survived the war intact, while many nearby towns and buildings were completely destroyed.

One terrible night two guests were staying with us at Kerzendorf. We had talked until late, when I called to my dog, Bibi, a long-haired dachshund that looked like a squirrel, to go out into the garden with me. What I saw made me catch my breath. In the stillness of the night gigantic globes of light were raining down from the sky, colored like precious rubies or emeralds,

8

more beautiful than anything I could ever have imagined. I stood transfixed, not understanding the meaning of the magic fireworks, when suddenly there was a terrible crash, followed by a huge geyser of sand and stones not far away. The earth rocked, the house swayed and people came rushing down the stairs. I brushed past them to fetch candles, matches and a coat, and stuffed everything I could lay my hands on in my room into its pockets. I was called down and hurriedly deliberated whether to stay on in the lightly-built cottage in which we were living, or to take refuge in the main house, which had stood empty since the beginning of the war, where the solid seventeenth-century vaults would offer greater protection. As we ran over the lawn, another blast threw us on our faces. Turning around I saw that the cottage was now sagging grotesquely to one side, while part of it had totally disappeared. When at last we reached the cellar, we were caught in a trap, for although the walls shuddered under the explosions, we dared not run into the open, where bombs might blow us to pieces. The roof over our heads caught fire. We clung together and prayed, all except my husband who went out to fight the flames and started to carry objects out into the garden under the fast falling incendiary bombs. As we implored him from the cellar entrance to come inside, he turned around indignantly and called back: "I care nothing for my life, I care only for my things." It was impossible to arouse in him a sense of self-preservation.

When finally the planes left, the water supply gave out, obliging us to stand for hours in front of the lovely old house, helplessly watching it slowly burn out, until nothing remained but its outer shell of yellow painted stone in the form of an eighteenth-century chest of drawers. Towards morning, holding the trembling Bibi in my arms, I turned away from all that remained of my childhood home, emptied of every feeling but relief that my parents were no longer alive to have witnessed the tragedy.

The next day a group of friends came out from Berlin to help

9

us salvage our possessions from under crumbled walls. Their sympathy momentarily eased our horror at the ugliness of the smoking ruins and the sight of crushed furniture and pictures. Yet as the cottage had not been directly hit, nor caught fire, but had collapsed under the blast of bombs falling around it, many of the things we disinterred were miraculously undamaged, and I was able to restore to their owners the objects they had put into my care. Most of them only survived four weeks longer, for they went up in flames at the house of a friend to which I had returned them.

As an empty gardener's house was the only building left standing, we decided to have part of it prepared for us to live in and we were impatiently waiting at Buckow for the necessary alterations to be completed, so that we could move back to Kerzendorf. Even though the house was now destroyed, the park we loved was intact with its grand old trees, planted in lines planned by the French landscape architect Blondel, a pupil of Lenotre's, who designed many German gardens of the middle-eighteenth century. From the front of the house we looked out onto a lawn bordered by poplars narrowing imperceptibly into a long avenue ending on the far horizon, while at the back of the house there was a corresponding alley. We lived in the centre of a harmonious work of art.

Buckow, our temporary refuge, was an old, solemn, square block of a country mansion built in 1700. There were no factories in its vicinity and at night a heavy fog arose from the surrounding lakes to envelop it in a protective cloud. Yet new and worse dangers such as revolution and invasion might replace the fear of air raids, for as the war progressed, security had ended everywhere, and we could not guess what form the final catastrophe would take. All we knew was that the war was lost and that the end was drawing near.

We had known war to be inevitable ever since 1933. The Party could not allow the revolutionary tension to slacken for a moment without the opposition immediately seizing its op-

10

portunity. Once the Secret Police was instituted, its system of denunciation destroyed all liberty of speech and action short of revolution, and it had become too late to act. The time had passed when the political parties like the Conservatives, the Catholic Centre Party and the Socialists, all headed by the ageing President Hindenburg, could have united to prevent the National-Socialists from coming to power. Instead, they had fought each other over minor issues.

One had but to look at photographs of the Nazi leaders to understand their lack of ability to govern a country whose geographical situation in the centre of Europe had always made its foreign policy an infinitely delicate task. None of their faces showed any spiritual quality, distinction or dignity, but all bore an expression of mixed bravado and of secret apprehension. Most of them were said to be sexually unbalanced, all lived at high tension from being continually on their guard against an ever-growing disapproval which they sensed, although they had officially silenced it. Despite their slogan 'The Reich we created will last a thousand years', they privately doubted whether it would even last their own lifetime, so that a fundamental feeling of insecurity removed their interest in long-term construction and gave them the insatiable greed of a pack of foxes in a farmyard, in a desperate hurry to grab and consume whatever they could. Some of us collected postcards of the Nazi leaders that were humorlessly sold at public booths, and would send one another grotesque photographs of Hitler wearing a forced martial expression, of Goering dressed in a fur cap and a shirt with lace sleeves, or of Goebbels shouting with an actor's grimace. We tried to convey to each other, 'Look how ridiculous they are, no one as phoney can touch us, their power will pass like the wind', yet underlying our amusement was a sense of horrified surprise that such unstable beings could have succeeded in disrupting our world.

Now that the consequences of their actions and character were being realized, we looked to 1945 with anxiety, for how would the drama evolve for us personally? We trembled at the approaching solution, yet we were determined to endure whatever lay in store for us, so that we could start anew on the other side of the gulf, and begin to live once more for our surroundings, instead of expending all our strength in negative opposition. In order to survive, it became necessary to weave a close web of thought, contemplation and calm around the vulnerable core of our being. Threads had to be woven into a chrysalis so enveloping that it was possible to remain intact within its protection, in the hope of emerging from its covering once the storm had blown over. But how would we react to unknown tests, perhaps too terrible for our strength, and capable of breaking our spirit by making us afraid? At moments courage failed me and I was overcome not so much by the thought of what could happen, as by the idea of losing my nerve, by an unconquerable fear of fear.

Chapter III

ONE DAY during our stay at Buckow, I went to Berlin to see my doctor. It was an exceptionally cold winter. For weeks the temperature had been many degrees below freezing-point, and while in normal times it took only an hour by train or car to travel to Berlin, it had now become a formidable expedition. When I left the warm house at five in the morning to cross the dark garden and went out into the icy streets poorly lit by dim lanterns, the delicate sickle of the moon stood in the sky and there was stillness but for the sound of my steps echoing in the hushed country town.

Trains arrived and left at odd hours, time-tables had ceased to exist with the continuous bombing of stations, and along with other travellers I sought refuge from the biting wind in a little wooden shack that served as a waiting-room. We were standing closely packed together, chilled to the bone, waiting helplessly for hours, when I felt someone cautiously pulling my coat sleeve. Turning round, I recognized the chauffeur of a diplomat who had been evacuated to a house near Buckow after his legation had been destroyed by bombs. He beckoned me to follow him outside onto the platform, where he took my hand, kissed it and said imploringly: "Will you believe me when I assure you I am a man of honour?" I was taken aback, for as I had only seen him twice from the rear seat of the car, I had never had the chance to probe his character. "I am in despair, without hope, without friends," he went on, and explained that he was one of the Spaniards sent to Russia with the so-called 'Blue Division', to help Germany fight Russia. After being wounded, he managed to free himself from his military engage-

13

ment by obtaining a driver's job with a diplomat—diplomats in those troubled times were set apart from ordinary mortals by their special privileges that gave them the power to protect and help. But now the whole Spanish regiment had been ordered back to the front, and the man's Embassy had bidden him obey orders. "The Russians are advancing," he whispered in terror. "They are sure to take me prisoner and shoot me. I know nothing about politics. I became a Falangist with a group of boys from my village. When I was sent here, none of us imagined that winters in Germany were so cold, the food so different to what we were used to, war so much more terrible than Civil War. I pray God day and night that I may not have to die in this foreign country. If you come to my rescue He will help you in your own troubles." He begged me to intercede with his employer, who was shortly leaving for Switzerland, to save him by taking him with him. I was disturbed at being confronted by a man in such agony of mind, and was relieved to learn some time later that he had succeeded in escaping.

In the light of early dawn Russian prisoners were standing and squatting on the hard, frozen floor. They had the Oriental gift of being able to drift off to sleep or semi-consciousness at any moment, with a lethargy that made them indifferent to the passing of time and to what went on in front of their eyes. The men looked dazed and sullen. The women were more lively and occasionally talked to each other. All were warmly dressed, but none wore shoes; their feet were bound in shapeless bundles of rags.

On the other side of the hut was a group of Polish-speaking people, among whom a young girl caught my attention. Her clothes were darned and patched in so many places that they were nearly falling apart. All her rags were of some shade of grey, and the only other tone was the faded pink handkerchief about her neck, so that in her utter state of destitution the girl's sense of taste and color was still apparent. When she and the man she was talking to came nearer I heard her cultivated voice,

14

and when she took off her rough glove I saw her thin-boned hand. She told me that she and the young fellow accompanying her were engaged, and that both were students from the University of Warsaw belonging to a resistance group which had been brought to work at this station. "We shall soon be able to go home," she said in a low voice. Then, as the relentless cold air was slowly lit by the rays of an ineffective sun, the overcrowded train came in at last to transport us to Berlin.

As most German aircraft had been destroyed during the Allied invasion of France in the summer of 1944, and since that time repeated air raids on factories had made the building of new machines in sufficient numbers impossible, there was almost no aerial defence of the capital. It was attacked every day. At the Zoo station, where we got out on reaching Berlin, no one had bothered to repair anything that was not vitally necessary for the running of trains, as it was certain to be destroyed again a few hours later. Doors stood awry, panes were broken, ticket machines were out of order. All one saw was soiled and broken. Only one counter was left open to serve the interminable queue of weary, shivering people whose faces were haggard from emotions roused by the dangers of the night. Disorder and neglect had eaten everything like leprosy; each step stirred up a thick cloud of dust composed of particles of shattered stones.

The same impression of dissolution struck me as I arrived at the hospital for my appointment with the doctor, where bombs had fallen only the night before. The house opposite was still smouldering, one on the other side was badly battered, the other had collapsed into a heap of rubble. I reached my destination by strenuously climbing over big blocks which obstructed the street, for the front door was damaged and visitors were obliged to use a side entrance. The electricity was not working, and I had to grope my way down a dark passage towards the waiting-room where I waited in the winter air streaming in through broken window panes.

15

An impassive nun wearing a large head-dress forming two white wings gently summoned me to the doctor. She lifted her downcast eyes to mine: "Our prayers have saved the hospital," she said. "Is there any surer proof of God's existence?" She led me to the window. "We alone were spared while the whole street was destroyed." Except for the building we were in, not one of the houses around had been left standing. The air raid had begun at midnight and when the patients had been brought down to the shelter, bombs and mines fell so thickly that doctors, nurses and patients believed their last hour had come. All the nuns had fallen to their knees in a group of fluttering whiteness and their steady murmur was heard through crashes and groans. When silence was restored, they found the houses next door in flames, but, as if by a miracle, not one spark had touched the hospital's roof. The story was spread through the stricken city.

The nun opened the door of the room occupied by the doctor, Maria Daelen. She was the daughter of a woman who had played a prominent part as a liberal member of Parliament, and was herself a fascinating and gifted woman of great beauty with large, blue-grey eyes and an expression continually varying between laughter and seriousness. For years she had always found means of helping or hiding people persecuted by the Nazis, either in her hospital or by a multitude of ingenious devices of which she alone knew the secret, and had done this with such dexterity that she had never been caught. That day she was pale and nervous from the terrors of the past night's raid, when her own apartment with all it contained had been destroyed while she was attending to her patients at the hospital. It was the fourth time that this had happened to her in the last few months, yet during our conversation she was telephoning to find another place to spend the next days in a casual way that showed how much we had learned to take insecurity for granted.

Ada, a mutual friend, was in the room with her. Her father

16

and husband were both held in a prison that as yet no one had ever left alive. We completely forgot the purpose of my visit in discussing the military situation. The end was approaching, we agreed, but would there be a joint final attack on the capital by all the Allies together? Who could tell? Ada was so consumed by hatred of the Nazis that she would not even consider it a misfortune if the Russians alone conquered the city. "Whoever comes is welcome to me," she said passionately, "if only they come quickly, before the Nazis have time to kill the two people I love. My greatest ambition is to arrive personally on a Russian tank at the entrance of the Lehrter prison and be present when my family is liberated."

I left them to go to the Buchholtz art gallery and bookshop. Although it had been bombed three or four times and many valuable objects had gone up in flames, Buchholtz, the owner, had indefatigably set up shop again and again, always in new buildings, and had collected new paintings or sculptures, so that the gallery was still the town's most important intellectual centre, as it had been during all the years since 1933. Buchholtz was too intelligent a man not to see the absurdities of current taboos, and thanks to his courage and to that of his young, good-looking assistant, who had the same serene belief in indestructible values, the atmosphere of the place never changed. The latter acted as host in the gallery in Buchholtz's absence and I can still see him climbing a ladder to reach a book with his long beautiful hands, or hear him making fun of a Nazi jury which vetoed sculptures before they could be shown in an exhibition. They would look at a nude of a boy and say: "This statue must not be presented to the public. The young man's body is too thin; it suggests that there is a food shortage in Germany." On the other hand, they would approve a heavily-built female figure because she looked capable of bearing many children.

Condemned pictures and sculptures, whether by foreign or by native artists, were carefully hidden in a little back room and shown only to those on whose discretion the owner could rely, for had he been denounced the gallery would have been closed and Buchholtz sent to a camp. Such rigid laws had been devised, that the painter Hofer was not only forbidden to show his work but had been denied the right to paint at all. Anyone seeing him with a brush in hand could have him sent to prison merely by reporting it to the Secret Police. Yet it did not deter him from going on with his work, nor the Buchholtz gallery from secretly buying his pictures.

As most boys and girls who grew up during that period never had an opportunity to see modern paintings, they were unaware of the visual conception of their own epoch. To the few students or young soldiers on leave who were taken to the Buchholtz gallery, the fresh point of view in art they discovered there for the first time acquired the fascination of forbidden fruit. The danger and the atmosphere of mystery surrounding what they came to admire, heightened their pleasure and endowed contemporary art with a charm that filled their imagination. It became symbolic of a freedom of self-expression which they were themselves denied.

Amongst books hidden behind a curtain in a corner, I found some by Gide and other banned authors, and Junger's *Marble Cliffs*, an allegory on the evils of a dictatorial government led by an ignorant revolutionary. As its allusions had escaped censorship, it had been widely read, until it had been forbidden some months before, not for its contents, but because Junger was compromised in the conspiracy against Hitler. I gave an order for some books to be sent to friends in prison, for perversely enough a bureaucratic system still permitted the imprisoned, even those doomed to die, to receive parcels and to exchange letters with the outside world.

Several plots had culminated in the unsuccessful attempt to assassinate Hitler in 1944. All connected with it were executed, together with many others who were not directly implicated, but who were found to have been involved in plans of their own to overthrow the régime. They had in every case unflinchingly risked their lives and died with great courage.

Various types of person had combated totalitarian methods and ideas, for men served the same cause in a different manner. Some, whose nature did not tend to violence, held and defended intellectual and spiritual positions, and it was for them and for the fire of their ideas that the militant revolutionaries were ready to risk all they had. It was for the approval of such dreamers aloof from action that they yearned, even after they had lost and knew they would die in vain. The rebels were inseparable from the thinkers who gave their sacrifice a meaning.

Many people were dissatisfied with the puerile ideology of the day, but the purely negative denial of its detractors seemed insufficient to those who were in search of lasting values on a higher level than obvious contradiction. Three different men who were a living antithesis to the reigning barbarism inspired their contemporaries, especially young men and girls, by their unshakable faith in human obligations. I cannot explain why it happened that they were all three Catholics, for their appeal was general and not religious.

One of them was Count Galen, the Bishop of Munster, who was of an ancient Westphalian family. He and the people of his diocese who mostly came of old peasant stock, understood and trusted each other because they had been brought up in the same tradition, shared with him a strong sense of their own dignity and knew how to be shrewd and stubborn in an identical way. The attempts of politicians to give them orders from the distant city of Berlin or of local officials to bully them, only made them smile incredulously. Galen's influence grew steadily as he calmly continued to preach his powerful sermons in which he denounced everything he considered wrong. Quite undeterred by threats, he wrote Pastoral Letters to exhort people to fight the evils of the time in the name of religion, and though there was a death penalty for reading them from the pulpit or for publishing them, it proved impossible to control their circulation from hand to hand in the form of typed leaflets. Their arrival was awaited impatiently. They were read, learned by heart and quoted all over the country, until finally the National-Socialist leaders decided that the Bishop's influence in Westphalia was so dangerous that his imprisonment was ordered. The Gestapo did not dare arrest him during the day when the population would have set up a struggle, and when they came for him at dead of night, Count Galen begged for a few minutes in which to dress himself, bidding them wait for him at the foot of the stairs. He then arrayed himself in his vestments, and with his mitre on his head, episcopal cross in hand, his golden surplice glittering and stiff about him, he descended the stairs in all his dignity to give himself up. When the unbelieving young men, who were in the pay of his enemies, saw the universally respected and loved Bishop coming towards them with his splendid assurance, they stared at him in startled awe and then fled in shame from the Episcopal Palace through an angrily gathering crowd. The next morning Munster and the whole province were seething with excitement. Telephones buzzed between the police and headquarters in Berlin, where a conference took place in which Himmler and Goebbels decided that an insurrection in Westphalia could not be risked during war. The Bishop was to be arrested as soon as it was won, they declared, and then be condemned as a traitor.

Another man whose personality and way of thinking were of great account amidst the desolation of an almost general silence due to exile, imprisonment and fear, was the writer and poet Reinhold Schneider. In one of the most memorable essays he published in the magazine *White Leaves*, he held up as an example of fortitude against persecution a Huguenot who had scratched the words 'Je maintiendrai' ('I will hold out') on the window pane of his cell in the fortress of Baux, where he had been imprisoned for his religious beliefs. The thin typewritten

20

sheets of paper were circulated, read and copied with a thrill of exaltation. His latest poems were sure to be passed around among the members of a small society called the 'Bibliophiles', consisting of a group of writers, doctors and scientists who met every fortnight in a long, dark room to hear lectures on historical or literary subjects. National-Socialism was never mentioned directly, but criticism of its despotism and hints of the transience of its power were made in clear allusions. The gatherings went on until the summer of 1944 when it became too dangerous for any group to meet, after similar bodies had been spied upon, dissolved and their members imprisoned.

Guardini, a Catholic priest of Italian extraction who wrote in German, had also exerted an outstanding influence. He had published books on Dostoievsky and Hoelderlin, a brilliant essay on Dante, and was then preparing his book on Plato. Since the war he had increased his activities, preached in a large church, spoken to students in a small hall, lectured on philosophical subjects, and received everyone who wished to consult him on matters of conscience. What he had to say was of such wide human import that Catholics, non-Catholics and atheists alike flocked to hear his speeches. His teaching reflected the sense of values developed by the Oriental, Greek and Christian civilizations towards which the social upheaval of our own times was creating a bewildering color blindness.

A young art student had asked him to read and explain Rilke's *Duinese Elegies* to a group of friends in his apartment, where we met regularly to listen to Guardini's clear explanations which made any obscurity of the poems vanish. Although we knew from his lectures that his own opinions were opposed to some of Rilke's non-Christian conceptions, he purposely kept his own personality in the background and interpreted the poet's meaning as a pianist would faithfully perform the work of a composer.

In wartime, youth and perfect health are the equivalents of mortal disease in peacetime. A man in full possession of all his faculties bears the tragic stigma of probable death in battle. When the charming and intelligent friend at whose house we had met was killed, his mother's reply to a letter of condolence was: "His loss is irreplaceable, but he is fortunate to leave this world of misery." This stereotyped answer which we had often heard during the past years was a reaction to conditions of existence that were becoming unrecognizable. Yet the boy who died might have carried the civilization which was his inheritance. The mother's defeatist reply was directly contrary to Guardini's teachings, who believed in the responsibility of every human being towards all others. Like Dante he would have banished those who gave up hope to the furthest corner of hell.

Renée Sintenis, the sculptress, was one of the few artists who had not fled to the country for greater safety. She had remained in an apartment which she would not abandon to its fate. Mounting to the top of the stairs of the house in which she lived, I passed floors now inhabited only by the wind blowing through shattered doors and walls.

In her room, attractive pictures caught one's attention, her small bronzes of animals stood on a shelf, the self-portrait of her tragic face with high cheek-bones, large eyes and full lips was on the table, a dog lay at her feet and a turquoise-colored love bird moved in its cage. For a moment I had escaped from the acid cruelty in which we lived. A mutual friend had just disappeared on the strength of an unproved denunciation, another had been sentenced to hard labour for a remark in a letter which the censor had opened. The sculptress' own life was difficult. She could not exhibit her work because it was claimed that her grandfather was Jewish, although she had proof that her grandmother had left her husband to elope with another man and had given birth to a child, who was Renée's future mother, before she could obtain her divorce and remarry. She could easily have sworn to it, as had others in similar situations, but without any show of heroism or giving a thought to the financial sacrifice involved, she never considered subjecting

22

herself to a demand which she deemed irrelevant to her art and disrespectful towards her family.

Renée was overwrought, in an agony of nerves from the ceaseless air raids, yet indefinably, her serenity even in suffering, her certainty as to what to admire, what to despise, was in such contrast to all around us that what was hard to bear became as insubstantial as clouds. She proved that human beings have the power to be beneficent as well as destructive, to produce happiness by the quality of their personality, even though they are at the limit of their own strength. Her incorruptible judgment, and the force of her indestructible gentleness, released one from the hypnosis of terror. Yet Renée did not seem to evoke faith by arguments or violence, it was her fleeting reactions, the sadness in her eyes as in the movements of her tall graceful person, her very existence, that conveyed spiritual encouragement and showed a way out of the labyrinth of hopelessness in which one was so easily lost. When I left her to walk slowly down the steep flight of stairs I felt richer than when I had come and was strangely consoled.

I had a luncheon appointment at the Hotel Adlon, the only place in Berlin where one could have a meal without being in acute fear of air raids. Cellars were no longer a protection, since bombs had been perfected to go straight through roofs, floors and vaults. On Hitler's orders special shelters had been built at the Adlon for the safety of foreign diplomats and for the high officials of the various ministries in the near-by Wilhelm-strasse. They were designed by the supreme authority on protective measures, Professor Speer, the Minister of Defence. Of the two different shelters constructed, as if for first and second-class passengers on a boat, the one for anonymous hotel guests, lying only a few yards underground, did not satisfy those for whom it was intended. When they saw the people deemed worthy of survival producing a pink ticket permitting them to take a staircase leading deep into the bowels of the earth, such violent scenes occurred that in practice nobody dared stop

23

anyone who forced his way down during the initial tension of an air raid. Once inside the hotel fortress, one felt less in danger than elsewhere. A medley of heterogeneous people stood about, noisily asking for tables and telephone calls, both obtainable by paying a currency of cigarettes. There was no daylight; electricity burned constantly in the lobby which was furnished with the heavy ugliness that flourished around 1910. The floor and the walls were covered by reddish marble ornamented with brass. Superfluous columns made a pretence of supporting the ceiling, chairs and tables were made of flimsy mahogany, all in the pseudo-luxurious setting that goes with large cigars and good brandy and with cheap taste in material and design.

While I waited endlessly for one of the tables that were overflowing into the lobby from the restaurant and bar, the white-haired Mr. Adlon, the hotel proprietor, came up politely and promised to get me one. He looked more distinguished than many of his guests, whose manners he complained of in a whisper, pointing out to me groups of loud Nazi officials in uniform wearing the short, unbecoming haircut that characterized them. Adlon significantly raised his eyes to heaven. "Waiters are also rude now, but," and he bent forward carefully, "how can they be different with these examples before their eyes?" and he pointed Abetz out to me, the Nazi ambassador to Paris during the occupation. "He looks like an ageing tenor," he remarked. "See how vain he is, how restless. But the house-painter Hitler has no idea of what a diplomat should be. It is an ordeal for me, a man who has known the era before 1914, to serve these uncultivated upstarts." It was not persecution or crime that shocked him, but the unbearable humiliation of being governed by a man whose humble origin he considered far beneath his own in birth and education. When I formed the word 'microphone' warningly, hardly moving my lips, he smiled with the superciliousness of a connoisseur, took the little table in front of us by its leg and tilting it, showed me that there was

24

nothing concealed beneath it. "Be careful of the central heating," he said with a slight wink. But we all knew that listening devices were built into the pipes, just as when we visited diplomats staying in the hotel they would begin by placing a cushion on the telephone, and if we wished to talk freely we murmured while leaning out of the window. "There are several machines in the walls and under the larger tables," he went on. "I cannot imagine how they hope to sift any valuable information out of the mass of contradictory material." Adlon looked about him. No one was paying attention to us. "Naturally the high Nazis' chief concern is in spying on each other, for now that the general situation is deteriorating, their distrust of one another is steadily growing. They have more to fear from enemies inside the Party than from outsiders who have become disorganized since the unsuccessful conspiracy."

We were interrupted by the melodious beat of a gong that conjured up a memory of the peaceful summons to a meal in a country house. As the dismal hooting of the siren did not penetrate into the lobby, Adlon had invented this polite device for warning his guests of the imminence of planes. It was in the same tradition that led Montaigne's father to have his young son awakened every morning by servants playing soft music outside his bedroom door, for he held it to be essential that the day's first impression should put the boy into a happy frame of mind instead of startling him into consciousness by an abrupt knock or a shrill bell. Yet although Adlon's civilized signal was less of shock than the sinister howl that sent a wave of panic racing through one's veins, the effect was the same: all of us, Mr. Adlon, the guests, waiters and bell boys started to move in a mass towards the staircase leading to the shelter, to push and scramble downwards on the damp steps.

Ants would have felt at home in the intricate network of underground passages to which we descended. Their pattern was conceived with the instinct of clever but limited insects, motivated entirely by fear. Not a detail diverged from this

25

one-tracked precept that excluded all fancy. A series of white-washed cells was furnished with rows of wooden benches and resembled classrooms; a voice from a loudspeaker monotonously announced the coming and going of planes in the skies above us in the droning tones of a schoolteacher. The endless corridors led far out under the Pariser Platz, for escape in case the hotel's exits were blocked, and the ventilator was so constructed that it would work even if the Adlon was struck. There was a reasonable chance of survival, yet our despair at being trapped, sometimes for two to three hours, grew with the knowledge that the capital was defenceless against the attacks that came day and night. But Party leaders knew themselves to be lost if they gave up the struggle, and thought only of prolonging their lives for a few miserable weeks. The more responsible of the army leaders had been liquidated for rebellion some months earlier, and the others were held back by Allies' demands for unconditional surrender, to which they would not submit before complete defeat. Meanwhile men died, cities were laid waste and women and children were helpless victims of relentless warfare. Weariness overcame me in the grim little room. I felt as if I were being compelled to read a detective story long after I had guessed its ending.

Conversations began between Italian, Spanish and Swiss diplomats, business people and various other guests who like myself had come to lunch at the hotel. Party members had congregated in a private room and were out of sight. A banker told me he was convinced that immediately after the war much money could be made in the rebuilding of the town. "The houses erected between 1880 and 1914 were so ugly," he said, "that except for the poor owners' loss it is lucky they are gone, for taste in architecture has now greatly improved, and Berlin may yet become a well-planned city. I am buying up uninhabited bombed houses in the hope of keeping them through the inevitable collapse of currency to sell them at a profit later on." Next to me sat a fair young woman carrying a spacious bag. "I never move without it," she remarked, "I don't wish to be taken unprepared by a long air raid, so when I go out, I take with me all I need to fight starvation and boredom." She showed me her little ration of sugar for condensed nourishment, brandy to keep up her spirits and the longest book she had been able to find, Tolstoy's *Anna Karenina*. I noticed a bundle of white sheets of paper. "Are you writing a novel?" I asked. She paused for a moment, then admitted that she was taking notes for an article entitled 'The Battle of Berlin', which she planned to smuggle out of the country to sell to a Swiss paper.

Drinks circulated, we waited on, talked and became very hungry, while the wireless reported dramatic fighting overhead, with parachutists jumping into space. We were told that two streets we knew well were destroyed in such casual accents that it sounded unreal in the prim little room.

We became silent and each of us relapsed into our newspapers, books or reflections. I thought of the last time I had been shut up here, which was in the beginning of July 1944 when two of the chief conspirators of the plot of July 29, 1944, had been present, at a moment when we knew nothing of their plans, although we were aware of their opinions. One was a tall man of thirty with dark hair and melancholy, intelligent eyes, who looked more like an intellectual than a revolutionary man of action. He had just returned from Switzerland where, with the connivance of his fellow conspirators, he had tried to ascertain what the American and British attitude would be in the event of the overthrow of National-Socialism. But as he had found it hopeless because of the rigid formula of unconditional surrender, he had decided that the only course was to negotiate with Russia. His friend, a fair young East Prussian landowner, had contradicted him vehemently: "No good can come out of an arrangement with the Soviets. It would only bring a new totalitarian influence." He said, "Besides it is too late. Peace with Russia was obtainable only before the fall of

27

Stalingrad in return for the surrender of the Ukraine and a recognition of the frontiers in Poland and the Baltic provinces as they were in 1942. Now they are too strong to need permission to take what they want and the only alternative is an agreement with the Western powers at any cost."

The dark man changed the subject to discuss Huxley's *Grey Eminence*. Like Huxley, he believed that men must lose themselves so deeply in their convictions as to be willing to die for them. "We will live to see martyrs in the world again. There will have to be a long line of believers to lead us through the darkness of tyranny to a future freedom. There is an important, an essential distinction between martyrs and victims," he urged. "The latter are passive, they appeal to pity, must be defended and avenged. The others are fighters; they consciously risk failure and death in their determination to rebel." Shortly afterwards we heard of their courage under torture and their death, and we were moved all the more by the memory of the words by which the two men had hinted at their destiny.

At last the welcome call of the gong released us and permitted us to return to daylight. All foreign diplomats repaired to a private dining-room, for it was Wednesday, the day on which Ribbentrop, the Minister of Foreign Affairs, summoned them to lunch every week at the Adlon. Embassies and legations had been pulverized in the course of the last year, so the foreign representatives had rented houses outside Berlin to elude constant danger and only came into town once every five or six days, to spend the night at the Hotel Adlon. Thus isolated, it was difficult for them to obtain political information and far easier for the Gestapo to watch over them and to keep track of whom they spoke to.

I joined some friends in the dining-room where they had settled in a corner, as far away as possible from a couple said to be agents of the Gestapo. Except for the man's repellent, cold fish eyes, he was a handsome fellow who had retained the outmoded elegance of a dancer just about to start a tango of

28

around 1925, the epoch when he had been young and rich. Now he had run into debt and was suspected of having offered his services as an informer. The pretty girl he was lunching with was divorced, and one of the diplomats was paying her much attention lately—imprudently, for she probably reported all he said. Both the man and the woman had a craving for luxury, and their frivolity was dangerous. Being devoid of conscience, they were capable of denouncing friends to the police. Their work consisted in making lists enumerating the associations of people they knew, and of repeating conversations they overheard.

Next to us sat a Spanish Duke, here on business, who had surprised us at first by his fluent German, until we learned that he had been an artillery officer from Düsseldorf. He had once made a trip to Madrid, where he met a Spanish lady, heiress to an illustrious name, who fell under the spell of his masculine charm. When they married, she had according to the custom of her country bestowed her title on him. Since then, when he said 'we', he meant the Grandees of Spain.

Several lively and well-dressed young women fluttered about the high officials and their adjutants in an effort to attract them, none of whom were in the least attractive. It was power, power alone, that made the pulses of the lovely creatures beat. Had they paused for a second, they would have realized how insecure was the position of the men around them and sensed the wind that had already risen to sweep them away. But the girls were aware only of the glittering glamour of uniforms, decorations and big flashing black cars, which they mistook for reality.

A little further on sat a young conductor with his wife. It was reassuring to look at him, for he was certain to be carried through to the future by his talent, sure to exist and develop long after the others had vanished into the obscurity out of which the passing whim of a revolution had temporarily lifted them.

After looking around I concentrated on my own table, where some attractive young couples were sitting. They were teasing Hans, Baron Lotow, who was engaged to a charming girl whom he was to marry in a fortnight. He said he intended to have a small wedding, to invite his family only, but no one present would hear of it. "You cannot do this to us," they pressed him. "Who knows how far away from each other we may soon be," we insisted, "we want you and your future wife to have a wonderful wedding in spite of the times, surrounded by us, your friends, and we beg you to let us all come together to see each other—who knows?—perhaps for the last time and be happy for a few hours." We assured him that we would contribute food for the buffet. One of us decided to arrange a lunch after the ceremony. Two Danish journalists offered to give a party on the evening of the wedding for the guests coming from outside Berlin. "But who will come? Who will be crazy enough to travel at the risk of being bombed on the train?" cried the bewildered bridegroom. We told him of friends who had already written to inquire about the marriage date, so they could plan their trip to coincide with it, of close friends who wished to come out of affection for him. They and acquaintances looked forward to a short respite from sombre tragedy. Hans finally gave in and laughingly promised to let us do as we wished.

It was time to take the train back to Buckow. The newspapers at the station were subject to Party censorship. No opinions were allowed that contradicted official views and this applied not only to politics but to the reviewing of books and plays. To get at the truth one was obliged to subtract, add and combine from the empty tirades which we glanced through with distaste, yet our instincts had been so highly developed to read between the lines that we learned more than a reader untrained in that particular art could have imagined.

It was dark when I arrived at the little country town of Buckow, emerging into a world so different from the ruined city whence I came. Houses were standing intact, bravely as in a stage set, there was no smell of charred wood, the air was free from the dust of broken stones and large snowflakes were falling softly, hushing voices and footsteps. The street where I walked was just an average, normal street, but just out of sight, right and left, where lines and contours were obliterated, dark abysses of horror lay yawning, hidden by the merciful night.

Chapter IV

ONCE IN the house I was sheltered from the snow, but it was scarcely warmer than outside. It was difficult to heat rooms with high ceilings and thick walls with only a scanty supply of coal.

A door opened and Bibi rushed to me with as much excitement as if I had come back from Hades. She was right. I had. Her joy, her sigh of satisfaction when I picked her up, called me back to earth from eerie shadows. My sister-in-law and my husband were listening to the wireless in a room far enough from the other inhabitants of the house for them to dare to turn on the 'Voice of America' and the B.B.C. It was strictly forbidden—the penalty was many years of hard labour, yet one took the risk for in contrast to the falsehoods or half-truths of National-Socialist propaganda, foreign broadcasts seemed endowed with mystic infallibility, enhanced by the measured tones in which events were announced, and were a relief from hysterical assertions and accusations. Among the great variety of stations one of the best was a weekly political survey by Professor Salis from Switzerland, while a British station called 'Atlantis' was especially popular with soldiers, for in addition to news it featured scandals about the Nazi leaders, comically told in coarse terms and expressions. Many local informers must have transmitted incidents to the British station as soon as they occurred, for the gossip was always only a few hours old and remarkably correct. It had great influence in detaching the confidence of the general public from National-Socialism by revealing the manifold weaknesses of its leaders. It was an open secret that no one owning a radio could possibly resist the temptation of turning the button just a quarter of an inch in order to hear a voice reveal oracular truth, but it would have been fatal to admit it.

A landowner in Silesia who had been denounced for listening to foreign broadcasts was summoned to the Gestapo, questioned and cross-examined. He denied the charge and it could not be proved. Finally, the Gestapo agent escorted him politely to the door and there said to him in a low, obsequious voice, "My dear Sir, of course we all listen to foreign news, but from now on you must promise to be more careful."

"I will," said the landowner, thereby trapped into admitting his crime. He was immediately arrested, condemned and disappeared into a camp.

A contrasting extreme of discretion was resorted to in a Catholic town in the Rhineland, where some unfortunate parents had received an official communication announcing the heroic death of their only son at the front. After some days of despair the British broadcast mentioned one evening a long list of German prisoners' names, and the parents heard to their indescribable relief that their own boy was alive. Meanwhile they had already arranged for a priest to read a mass for the benefit of his departed soul and invited all their friends to attend it. The priest, as it happened, had listened to the same broadcast, as well as the whole congregation, and the next morning the young man's mother received about a hundred anonymous letters telling her that her son was alive. Yet they could not cancel the ceremony without being compromised, so the mother appeared in church dressed in flowing weeds, the father was a study in black, as was the sister, except for a little white line at her neck, and although there were no heartrending tears, faces were absolutely solemn. The Priest's sermon was about the raising of Lazarus from the dead, and he pointed out that in every extremity there was always room for hope.

The worse the military situation, the more pitiless were the measures taken to stop the circulation of bad news. The machinery of everyday life began to break down even in the backwaters of Buckow, when suddenly, for no visible reason, the electricity ceased to work. 'Sabotage', people whispered under their breath. The electric train leading to Berlin stopped running and the local factories stood still, leaving the workers to walk home moodily, talking and conjecturing. One afternoon when friends from Berlin came to visit us in the car of a Swiss diplomat they brought along a twenty-one-year-old German officer on leave who had been drafted only recently. He was indignant at what he had seen at the front where the offensive in the Ardennes had just begun. "It is a hopeless venture," he said, "without the slightest chance of success. Thousands of lives are being sacrificed so that Nazi leaders may keep their positions a few weeks longer." He then repeated what we were now hearing from all sides: "Why not give up the War in the West and concentrate all troops towards the East?" He went on to voice his own doubts. What should he do? Instigate a plot, a revolt? Try to desert?

The others were talking about life in the capital in the intervals of bombing. Many Nazi officials realized the end of their rule was near, and wished to escape before it was too late. Foreign diplomats were offered the release of political prisoners in exchange for passports, begging the permission to sell human beings so that they could flee from the revenge they feared. They tried to forget their anxiety in wild diversions and gave parties every night. One, that had taken place at the Croatian Legation the evening before in a large house in the Grunwald, began as a formal dinner for the head of the German press but ended in confusion when the guest of honour became so drunk that he pulled a pistol out of his pocket and shot at the electric light bulbs in the chandelier, narrowly missing a fellow guest.

As usual the conversation returned to the military situation. After the landing in France in June 1944 we had believed the war would end in three months, yet now at the end of the year

34

it was still going on. Six months, ten months, seemed interminable to those who were anxiously waiting.

The day of the 31st of December dragged heavily. We tried unsuccessfully to forget the date that conjured up memories of happier times, but we were unable to ignore it intentionally, as it had been easy to do in other years. In 1944 we were in the midst of an earthquake; the ground trembled under our feet; the coming months would perhaps bring us anything, liberation or destruction, life or death. Every single day starts a new year, yet who thinks of it on an 8th of April or a 3rd of August unless it is some anniversary? It is a blank page, virgin of remembered impressions, ready to be filled by new signs of life. Christmas, January 1, bring back a series of precise scenes, at every minute of the day we recall a vanished setting, a gesture or a conversation in a maddening torment of nerves and feelings.

These impressions grew in talking to a former servant of my parents who had come to spend his holidays in Buckow. Lately he had been serving at official dinners in Goering's house. One evening, at a reception for sober-minded business men, Goering had startled the company by appearing in shorts of gold leather ordinarily used for shoes, a toga, sandals revealing toe-nails painted red, an emerald here and there, a large diamond on the hilt of his sword, and accompanied by his pet, a lion. "His face was made up with brown paste, and there was blue cream on his eyelids," said Otto, his eyes wide with surprise.

After we had dined quietly, talking of trivialities, everyone dispersed, except my husband and myself who stayed up to listen to the wireless. The village church bells had been melted down for munitions during the past year, so we tuned in to a Swiss station at midnight. There was a pause, then the chimes began as if from quite close, although the bells were calling us from beyond an iron frontier, uniting us with the world beyond.

Outwardly there was nothing sombre on that 1st of January, 1945. The sky was a brilliant blue, and the sun gleamed on the snowflakes falling softly from the sky. The morning mail reminded us of the terrible general situation. A friend in East Prussia, who lived in a beautiful house which had been in her family for generations, wrote how she feared the Russian advance and its consequence. A jar of honey from Silesia was accompanied by: "The last I shall ever send you from home"; and another from a business man in Budapest which had taken three weeks to arrive described a long evening spent in a gay restaurant listening to intoxicating gypsy music. Now the wireless was monotonously relating details of the desperate street fighting in that same city. It went on to report a disastrous air raid over Berlin the previous night which had destroyed entire streets. Then, cutting into the enumeration of tragedies, one more sinister than the other, there came a shallow and embarraised New Year's address in Hitler's strangely hoarse voice. A maid arriving at that moment repeated the current rumour: "He has cancer and will soon die." We felt that that would have been no solution at this stage, and that the man whom we held responsible for the catastrophe should himself preside to the end and not be allowed to shift the responsibility of his actions on to others.

I opened two parcels containing books which had been sent to me as presents. One was Bromfield's *Wild is the River*, the other *Choses Vues*, the memoirs of the old poet and politician Victor Hugo in the throes of his rebellion against Napoleon III. In turning the pages I found that they dealt with many of our own central problems, particularly with political hatred and evil personified in one or a few single human beings. Hugo's opinion was that hate in any form, including hate for personal reasons, was an obsession irrevocably leading to a permanently arrested development. According to him men became powerful more through the defenders' weakness than by their own strength; they were blind instruments of an historical situation. It was the ideas one fought that mattered, not individuals, who once eliminated should be forgotten.

36

Existence at Buckow was of a deceptive peacefulness to which the constant flow of news of the decisive Russian offensive in the south of Poland, and recent events in Hungary and Austria were a gloomy accompaniment as well as a warning of what was coming ever nearer. The narrator on the wireless was like the man behind the scene of a marionette-theatre explaining the play to an unseen audience, while we were helpless and unwilling puppets anxious to awake from an everlasting nightmare.

To escape from my feelings of oppression, I went for solitary walks. The sky on these winter afternoons contained delicate pastel colors of pink and silver, the countryside was veiled by a light mist and every branch was studded with diamonds. At sunset a sudden breath dramatically blew out the light, stones and plants paled as the house changed from warm yellow to a bluish transparency and the light of the moon silently washed over reds and greens, turning them into slate-grey, clothing them with phosphorescent tones of driftwood and bones that spoke of the formlessness of death.

Nervous restlessness filled the next few weeks, and the difficulties of our daily existence increased as a result of the Russian advance. Half of the house in Buckow had been inhabited by members of the Rumanian Legation from the time when their house in Berlin was burnt, until Rumania had made peace with the Allies, when its representatives had either escaped to Switzerland or been interned as enemies by the Nazis in a small Silesian health resort. If other diplomats did not now take over their apartment, a party organization was sure to requisition it and we would be obliged to live under their odious supervision in constant fear of denunciation. There was consternation when a telephone call came from Ribbentrop to say that the entire remaining diplomatic corps had been ordered away to Gastein in Austria, and that the empty rooms were to be used by the Foreign Office itself. Several months before a large part of its staff had been evacuated from Berlin to a place in Silesia for fear of being bombed in the Wilhelmstrasse. Now the Russian Army was advancing in that direction, employees and truckloads of papers had been hastily moved to Buckow, oddly enough accompanied by a regiment of Cossacks who had never conformed to Bolshevism, and had been employed in fighting their own people on the German front. As the telephone service was constantly interrupted and petrol so scarce that there was not enough for official purposes, the Cossacks were to gallop from Buckow to Ribbentrop's country house, a three hours' riding distance, bearing messages back and forth. When news of the romantic Barbarians' expected arrival spread in the little town, it caused a tremor of delight among the girls, who looked forward to dancing and gaiety and hoped the strangers would bring a much desired stir of amusement into their young pleasure-starved lives. But when the shy, battered little men arrived a few days later, frightened and ill at ease, they were a great disappointment to Buckow womanhood.

When the minor officials of the Foreign Office arrived, they created confusion and resentment by demands that seemed out of place and senseless now that the Eastern Front was so close that the wind blowing from that direction bore with it the faint sound of machine-guns. A comment on this, or the slightest suggestion that Buckow was not an ideal choice as a permanent centre for important government offices, would have been considered treason, punishable by death. Forced activity continued in which no one believed, but it remained unquestioned.

One day we received a message from Kerzendorf telling us that the gardener's cottage was ready for us. What we had looked forward to for months had come true. At last we could go back, live by ourselves and be at home again. But late that night came a disturbing telephone call from a friend in Berlin: "A decisive event has occurred. I will tell you the news at Hans' wedding. Be sure to come." We were interrupted by a strident air-raid warning over the wire from Berlin. The telephone went dead as the line was cut, and we tried in vain to guess what had occurred.

Next day we passed through Berlin on our way from Buckow to Kerzendorf. On coming up the steps of the underground to the daylight, I was shocked by the grimaces of abandoned buildings, by the ruins of the last disastrous bombings, and the streets now empty of traffic. A few shivering people walked by quickly, muffled up against the intense cold, as drab and sad as their surroundings. Although all life seemed extinct, every one individually was full of spirit. The city was like a snake of which the parts continued to live after it has been cut into small pieces. A vivifying spiritual current made it resist being killed outright. I went to a telephone booth to resume the interrupted conversation of the day before and used the private code some of us had developed to a fine art for writing or telephoning. We spoke of England as 'Sybil', because of an English friend we had chosen to represent her country in our eyes, of Russia as 'Pit'.

Translated from our language, the news was that the military situation had become so hopeless that the final blow might come at any moment, for the Russians had broken through the German defences in three vital places. Although what was now imminent had for long been inevitable, I tried in vain to imagine the consequences of what I had been told. My mind went blank, leaving me concerned only for the most immediate problems.

As there was no answer to the telephone in our little apartment, I went there quickly. Hedi, a friend who was looking after it, was staying there with Pauline, a life-long servant of a dead aunt whom we had brought there after her house was burned down. Three air raids had taken place in the last twenty-four hours and like everyone else in town the two women were in a state of nervous prostration. They told me that Renée Sintenis' house had been blotted out, her pictures, bronzes, furniture and clothes were lost, her life saved by a miracle.

In my own room a large new crack and the absence of window

39

panes let in a winter cold so bitter as to make it agony to stay there. A Princess Biron of Courlande who had just arrived from Silesia came to see me. She had escaped from Breslau by climbing in through the window of a train packed with panic-stricken people. Her face was filled with terror as she related how Silesia had been swamped with the people driven forward by the Russian Army from the Polish frontier. They had filled the trains and roads, which shortly afterwards were swollen by the thousands of Silesians fleeing in their turn. She herself, like all her friends, had been forced to leave her house on her estate, without saving any belongings. Rape was a word that occurred again and again in her conversation. It was an expression which caused no pang of fear in our times for its meaning was purely figurative—'to be ravished' belonged to the realm of lyrical poetry. Now its original sense was terrifyingly restored and brought us face to face with a new peril.

In the same breath she told us of a party she had attended the evening before, the first one given in connection with Hans' wedding, where there had been a lot to drink and an excellent band, 'the Cuban Boys'. Around ten o'clock the siren broke up the festivities with its harsh warning. While the guests hesitated and time was wasted in deciding where to take shelter, blast shook the house. As it was too late to leave, the orchestra played louder, all joined in the dancing and singing to drown out the sound of explosions, to drink and forget, until the deafeningly sharp whistle of a fire-engine penetrated into the hot room. They looked out. The attack was over, but the house next door was hit, was on fire and the flames lit up the whole neighbourhood.

On the day of the marriage a lunch had been arranged in a little restaurant, for not one of the large group of friends had an undamaged room where it might have been given. We walked there through rows and rows of silent, uninhabited streets. Houses no longer served a human purpose, but had been reclaimed by nature to assume a weird beauty of their own. Jagged corners of façades cut into the blue frosty air, quadrangles that had once been windows now framed fleeting clouds, moving while all else was lifeless. The emptiness took on the pathos of a stage two seconds before the hero is expected. One saw through the crumbled walls to the distant canal beyond the streets and squares that had been the centre of the antique dealers whose shops were now destroyed and their owners ruined.

We believed we had missed our way in the midst of this desert, when a slim young woman wearing a little hat covered with bright feathers appeared out of nowhere, while another attractive girl and some handsome young men came along in search of the restaurant where we were to meet, accompanied by a couple of Hungarian refugees from Budapest who wore picturesque brown-frogged leather coats. The large car of the Spanish Ambassador drove up, and as he got out with a number of people whom he had brought, they looked incongruous amidst the desolation around. Yet when at this moment chance passers-by appeared on the scene, they called out a few friendly words of greeting. There was no irritation or envy in their eyes at the sight of the colorful group, only relief, for like us they were in revolt against overpowering ugliness. The visible evidence of the indestructibility of youth and charm appealed to an instinct of self-preservation. It gave the same pleasure as the first sign of spring, as a cluster of violets on a wintry day.

The only house standing for miles around contained a restaurant reserved on that day for the luncheon party of forty people who were all in high spirits at having succeeded in snatching a little cheer from the forces of darkness. No sooner did we sit down than the weird sound of an air-raid warning drove us inexorably to a shelter. We took it as a matter of course, as a trivial part of our momentary existence, and did not permit it to interrupt our conversation. Any remarks about so familiar an experience would have been obvious, repetitious and in bad

41

taste, so we returned to resume our meal as if the interval had been a normal event—which indeed it was.

The wedding reception took place later in the afternoon in a hotel situated in a street that had taken on an unfamiliar air in the complete blackout. Its tightly shuttered houses wore a menacing look, and we stumbled at every step over the deep holes torn into the pavement. For some time we could not find the entrance to the building and looked for it helplessly in the bitter wind, until a door opened and we were ushered from the cold and gloom into a brilliantly lighted room, into the midst of an animated crowd surrounding and congratulating the bride and bridegroom.

It was surprising how some of the guests present had escaped the vigilance of the Gestapo, especially a Baroness Gerstorff, at whose home the conspirators of July 20 had met daily. Her husband's and her connection with these men was well known, yet it seemed to have been hidden by a cloak of invisibility. They had never been interrogated or molested, while many other innocuous people had been sent to concentration camps for a mere overheard remark.

One of those present was an attractive Austrian girl, a Princess S., who had been a friend of the conspirators, yet she was not implicated and after its failure had obtained permission to visit the prisoners. Two of her brothers had disappeared after the capture of Stalingrad. It was persistently rumoured that the Russians had permitted German prisoners to write to their families through Turkey and Switzerland. Hitler had ordered the letters to be held back, for he feared that at this hopeless stage of the war, evidence of Russian kindness towards prisoners would act as an incentive to German soldiers to desert. The girl obtained an appointment with one of the generals, and implored him to have the mail looked through to see if it contained news of her brothers. When the general admitted the existence of letters and told her that they had been destroyed unread, she lost her head and expressed her contempt for his refusal to help in the killing of a leader who had brought nothing but disaster. The general was secretly an active member of the conspiracy, so this violent attack was a shocking blow to him and he could not guess if the girl were indiscreet or if she were trying to compromise him, to endanger the success of the plot. As soon as she left him he got in touch with the other conspirators and they decided it was necessary to have her done away with immediately. But luckily, two of those whom the general consulted were acquainted with her, and by vouching for her, succeeded in saving her life.

The Gestapo's inefficiency resulted from its management by men who were not only ruthless, but ignorant and submerged in masses of contradictory information. The conspirators were constantly seen in each other's company and none of them had ever hidden their hostility towards the Fuehrer and his policy. Yet they were allowed to continue their trips to Switzerland quite undisturbed until the day when their bomb exploded, and instead of eliminating the man they hated, brought destruction on themselves. On looking around I felt with a shiver to what extent survival was a matter of luck. The fiancé of a girl who sat a few feet away had been dragged off to prison a month ago because his secretary had overheard him make a disparaging remark about Hitler and he had now been sent to the front in a 'Death Squad', where the fighting was so dangerous it amounted to a death sentence.

When I went to take leave of the bridal couple I found them in worried deliberation, for they did not know where to spend their wedding night. The window panes in the bridegroom's apartment had been blown to pieces the evening before, like those of the upper floor of the Hotel Adlon where they had obtained a room. Both alternatives were unpleasant, as it was below freezing-point, but there would have been no other choice if a compassionate friend had not put his own room at their disposal for a few days.

It was about nine o'clock when we left to go on to the party

43

which two young Danish journalists were giving at an art dealer's attractively furnished flat. They had borrowed this room for the evening since their own apartment had been destroyed the day before. As we entered, the two hosts distributed tickets to us, on each of which was typed the name of the person with whom we were to drive off to a shelter in case of an air raid. They had divided us so that there would be exactly five people in every car. "For I hate a panic," one of them said earnestly. I asked him the burning question: "Is it true that the Russians have broken through in three places?"

"In three?" he answered, "at least in twenty-five."

One of the guests was a Silesian landowner who had come to the capital on business and who was in acute anxiety about the future of his country estate to which he was returning the next morning. "I hope to have three more weeks there," he said despairingly. He had anticipated the present government's catastrophic failure with such certainty that in 1933 he had acquired a small farm in Brazil. But although he could easily have sought refuge there, it was unthinkable for him to abandon his home where he had grown up, as had his ancestors before him, unless he were driven out by force. He felt personally responsible for the welfare of the people he had known since childhood and felt part of the landscape. As only violence could separate him from the land which owned him as much as he owned it, he was resolved to go back to face all eventualities. We were both overtaken by a wave of dread. Only this evening's light and companionship separated us from unimaginable perils each of us would have to fight alone. A gramophone started to play, and dancing went on wildly, incessantly, until early morning, uninterrupted by air raids. No one wanted to hear more news or know anything of the future beyond the short hours of the night.

The planes which for unknown reasons had refrained from coming in the evening arrived in full formation the following morning and filled the air with a roar that belied their clear-cut

44

elegant outline against the sky. As soon as the warning sounded I fled to the nearest shelter, to the gigantic windowless tower resembling a formidable medieval Roman fortress called the Zoo bunker. Ominous machine-guns pointed from its roof and streaks of green paint on its grey walls gave it a beautiful shade of copper patina. It served both as a storage place for the safe-keeping of art treasures from the museums and as a protection for human beings. Bombs had fallen on it repeatedly without loosening a stone.

Anyone leaving Berlin would say to the person he loved: "Swear to run to the Zoo bunker as soon as an air raid begins," and go away reassured if the promise were given. I felt safe there, yet on entering its dark interior, claustrophobia took me by the throat. In the dim half light of two barnlike rooms the huge staircase connecting them was filled with an anonymous crowd of indistinct shadows in Purgatory, by a mass of twenty thousand people seething up and down restlessly, talking nervously in a steady murmur. As usual I carried a book in my pocket, but reading was impossible, for you were pushed, jostled and deafened by a harsh voice booming news through a loud speaker for many hours. When release came and I went out of the large doors, I could not open my eyes because the blinding clouds of smoke came from houses burning on the opposite side of the street. I groped my way back slowly and painfully along a wall until I reached the square where our house, much to my surprise, had escaped destruction.

A visitor was waiting for me at home, a girl of twenty, a gifted writer, who had come to show me some poetry she had written and to complain about the behaviour of a man she wanted to marry. Nothing of what was happening around her disturbed her in the least, for she was too absorbed in her own problems to care. Five years of war were so long a part of her short existence that she could not remember conditions before it started very clearly, and took all accidents of the time for granted. Although they were unpleasant to her as the bitter

45

cold surrounding us, she knew by instinct and without impatience that they would not go on for ever and expected their end with the same certainty as the coming of summer.

I went to lunch at a restaurant next door. At a table near mine there was a group of young Frenchmen with a compatriot of theirs married to a Hungarian, who had abandoned her and their little girl without a cent. She had been prevailed upon to write for Vichy newspapers to make a living, and I gathered from her companions' conversation that they also were journalists working for the collaboration. All showed great anxiety. "We are lost, where can we hide?" they whispered. "We will be imprisoned and shot when they catch us."

The woman said: "I could find no other work to do, or so I thought." "Do you regret it?" one of the men asked. She answered in a voice of such misery that I was startled: "Life is nothing but a calvary."

An order had been issued stating that all clothes not absolutely necessary to their owners were to be turned over to the State. Everything collected was to be ground in a mill to produce new material for soldiers' clothing which they needed for the hard Russian climate. Offices had been especially installed, where party members with shiny badges sat under their red Nazi flag checking what was brought to them. Men were not to keep more than one suit, women as little as possible. Denunciation might bring a general requisition of the household possessions. As all our useful clothes had long since been given away, all I had left were discarded evening gowns, dominoes or fancy dresses I had forgotten about which brought back to me happy evenings on which I had worn them. As I added a sweater to them and handed them to a severe-looking woman with tightly compressed lips, a man standing in the queue behind me said so softly that she could not hear him: "Why don't you give me that jacket? You don't really believe soldiers will get it?" We were told later that all the things had disappeared among the minor party members who had taken charge of them, just as had happened a year previously when skis were ordered to be given up for use in the Russian campaign. But people had now become tired of continual sacrifice and they brought their clothes ungraciously, with sullen faces. One woman muttered: "The government has taken my husband away from me, why should I have to give them his pants as well?"

On the way to the station for Kerzendorf we passed Rothe's flowershop that used to be a feature of Berlin in peacetime. Rothe decorated his display windows with color combinations of exquisite flowers that were an enchantment to passers-by. He was standing in the almost empty shop when I went in. "Our last standing hothouse was bombed yesterday," he related in a flat voice. "It is a tragic loss, for now I can grow no more plants. Here is one last orchid"; he showed me a branch covered by a row of yellow blossoms hovering over it like exotic butterflies. "This is no time for creations as delicate as these," he continued sadly, "nor for music or any of the arts of peace. Grace has fled the country, and all the little things that have made life worth living are fled with it."

At last we found a seat in the train, despite its being filled by Polish, Ukrainian, French and Belgian workers returning to Ludwigsfelde, the little town near Kerzendorf, where they had been brought from all over Europe to work in the Daimler factory. It was generally believed the men and women employed there would take violent revenge by murdering and burning all they could lay their hands on once they were free to retaliate. On that day some of them seemed apathetic and dejected, while others carried on animated conversations in low voices.

An old carriage drawn by an ancient horse and driven by an aged one-eyed coachman awaited us at the station in Ludwigsfelde. The coupé there had belonged to my grandmother, was shabby from old age but retained its clean lines and elegance. The covering of dark green leather emitted a special fragrance and reminded me of my childhood, when a row of vehicles

47

stood unused in the stables. There were open victorias for fine weather, light traps for country drives and roe-buck stalking, coaches for driving four-in-hand. Now they had been turned from daily conveniences into derelict museum pieces. The throbbing machines in the garage next door were alone thought worthy of attention while the carriages in all their fanciful variety were left to moulder in the dark, forgotten except by children who delighted in climbing in and out of them. At last one of their long row had come to life again, now that there was no petrol to feed fast cars.

Chapter V

As we drove along the road, the grass was scorched black in places from fire and in others there were enormous cavities where bombs had ploughed into the ground. We reached Kerzendorf, and entered the cottage where we were to live. Between the white and gold panelling of the library, flames crackled busily in the open fireplace and an eighteenth-century portrait of a haughty Duke of Hesse, wearing a red velvet coat crossed by the light blue ribbon of an order, smiled in welcome to us from over the mantelpiece. My own room had been painted grey, and there were grey taffeta curtains on the windows. A portrait of my grandmother as a young woman dressed in white satin with three rows of coral around her neck hung on the wall, and the light, dancing on the red books, repeated the color. "You must get a red or a white dressing-gown," remarked my husband, looking around. "Any other tone would be impossible."

The incessant rain of bombs in the city did not frighten Freddy, but it was so difficult for him to submit passively to a political situation which his sane judgment could not accept that he completely changed his mode of existence. Instead of living in a crowd of people, he now decided to make our home a retreat as remote but also as attractive as possible. He put all his energy into creating a sort of Noah's Ark in which he proposed that we two should survive.

The day of our arrival was unbelievably cold, the house had been uninhabited for a long time, the walls were icy to touch and covered with drops of moisture. But there was plenty of wood for the stoves to overcome the dampness, and in any case the temperature seemed of no importance to us. Foremost in our minds was gratitude at being home again and nothing could lessen the bliss that filled our hearts.

In the middle of the night we were awakened by a wheezy, irritating sound like that of an overgrown mosquito. Could it be? Yes, it was the call of a little trumpet warning us of approaching planes. We dressed quickly, then hastened through the farmyard at the back of the house to a narrow, windowless vegetable cellar constructed partly underground, its interior resembling a street car, that served as an air raid shelter for the peasants and various people who lived around. I took Bibi on my lap and we reassured and warmed each other in the endless hours of the freezing night.

Opposite me sat a woman refugee who had been driven from a village in the East. Her mind was occupied during the day, but while sitting at leisure in the dark, her hands in her lap, grief over the abandoned house took hold of her. Unaware of who was listening, she enumerated her losses in a moaning soliloquy, found words of endearment for cows and hens, for the fruit trees in the garden, for her bees and flowers. She recited and repeated the list of her former possessions in a haunting chant while rocking herself backward and forward in an agony of home-sickness.

When bombs fell in our vicinity we realized how flimsy our roof was. Our long standing wish to settle in Kerzendorf had been fulfilled, but an ironic destiny had granted it at a moment when the strain of constant danger was darkly mixed into every second of enjoyment.

The next days were filled with activity in preparing to receive refugees from East Prussia. They arrived sick from the long trip in unheated trains, in weather so exceptionally cold that small children died on the way. Friends passing through Berlin telephoned us in despair at having been torn from their homes. They were going as far west as they could, and while we did all we could to console them, we felt the threatening storm had almost reached our own doorstep. In contradiction to what

50

was happening to others, we were making our own house liveable.

My husband decided we must arrange it perfectly. The old carpenter who was as passionately interested in interior decoration as my husband came out from Berlin. Together they hung pictures on the walls, and arranged the furniture. When they started to put up a pair of eighteenth-century curtains of yellow coloured tapestry, I protested. "Why should they remain hidden in a case?" Freddy defended himself. "If anything should happen either to me or to them, I will at least have had the pleasure of enjoying them until the last minute."

I left them to their occupation, while I visited our nearest neighbours at Lowen. They had invited me to meet the young man engaged to the grand-daughter of the old lady who was the owner of Lowen. I rode over in the rickety little carriage, driven fast by the coachman who was afraid of being caught in an air raid while on the road. On entering the old house and seeing the family assembled there, I was transported into a world in which the events of the day had not as yet penetrated and where no disturbing questions were admitted. Chairs and sofas of a touching Victorian pompousness, clumsy golden chandeliers and mirrors seemed fixed on the walls for eternity. It was an army milieu, not Nazi but nationalistic, where National-Socialism was not disapproved of for its foreign policy or its persecutions, but for its Socialist tendencies. Yet they had never formally opposed it because Hitler, through rearming, had favoured and enlarged the army to which they were primarily attached. Positions had been created in the new military formations in which many people with whom they were connected had found a living suitable to their tastes and talents. The outbreak of hostilities in 1939 did not shock them, for they considered war a natural activity for the human male and a better solution for political quarrels than negotiations. They had started to oppose Hitler only recently, since the generals had revolted and had been executed. Ideas were no concern of theirs; it was the attack against their class, which they felt to be the salt of the land, which had aroused their resentment. Yet although they were now in opposition, their obedience to an established order as well as national pride would not let them admit to defeat in war. In listening to them one wondered if they were blind to reality or if they only pretended to ignore it. At this moment, when it was obvious to every child that the war was lost, they appeared to be full of confidence in victory and spoke of newly-invented weapons that would turn the tide.

When I was told of the plans for the girl's wedding at the end of February on her parents' large estate in Silesia, near the Polish border, I remarked rather diffidently that according to the news heard over the wireless on that day, January 19, 1945, the date seemed far off and dangerous. It was taken very badly.

"What do you mean?" they said disapprovingly. "How can you doubt the success of our great army and its valiant leaders? It is not as though the country were defended by those low-born Nazis alone. Generals and officers will certainly not let invaders in any further than they have to for strategical reasons, so as to beat them with all the more certainty."

They considered my objections defeatist and unpatriotic and refused indignantly to accept them.

"All the neighbours have already been invited. Of course the marriage will take place there and the young couple will spend their honeymoon on another estate in that district."

I was amazed to see them living in a world of delusions. As soon as I gave up contradicting, I felt the atmosphere grow pleasant again, for in their minds everything flowed on uninterruptedly towards a future that was an image of the past. They believed in the importance of family life, of friendship, of personal relationships. Their physical courage, their sense of duty were beyond doubt, but their great virtues were marred by ambition and kow-towing to authority at the cost of their sane judgment.

Tea was served. The girl was happy, her fiancé charming;

they talked of their home in Silesia as though it were in no way menaced, until I felt I were taking part in a play.

I lingered, but the coachman sent in an excited message to say that an air raid was impending. We had to depart hurriedly before the planes arrived, leaving my hosts serenely prepared to go to the cellar. We galloped along the dark road to reach the house just in time to obey the creaking trumpet by running to the shelter. Even the official news issued by the Nazis now became clearer in its portent, for although claiming victories in blustering tones, towns mentioned in bulletins were further inside Germany each day and indicated the Allied advance.

A Baroness Blumen telephoned to announce her visit in the afternoon on her way to Hamburg from her estate in Pomerania. A few hours later she arrived with a large group of people in diplomatic cars, filling the quiet house with bustle. She told us how refugees had been arriving at her country house for weeks, relating stories of horror about the Russians. When she had decided not to risk staying on and had made up her mind to leave, she went through her house taking stock of all it contained. After filling her car with the few belongings she deemed indispensable, she gave word for the inhabitants of her village to assemble. Standing in front of her house she made a speech to tell them she wished to distribute her possessions among them before departing, and gave away all the furniture, china, linen, everything the large, well-stocked house contained that she could not take with her.

"I like acting spontaneously," she declared. "I made sure that friends and people in need got my things instead of thieves intoxicated by looting." Then she addressed herself to me.

"I have come to say goodbye to you."

We both thought without expressing it: "Will we ever see each other again?" and secretly doubted it.

"You do not really think of remaining here?" she asked incredulously. My affirmative answer gave me a sharp pang of uneasiness. Everybody was seeking safety, we alone had just

53

arrived in Kerzendorf and had made no plans whatsoever for protection.

A Hungarian, who was one of the party, related details of what had happened in his country when it had been invaded by Russians a few weeks back. The Croat minister interrupted him by saying that every victorious army behaved in the same way, that this as well as the Soviet system itself were transitory, for if its excesses had been a necessary evil to impose a revolution by force, it was certain to pass and the real Russian nature would reassert itself.

"Europe has arrived at a dead end, at a stalemate, for having become purely materialistic," he argued. "Fascist inhumanity was only possible because no inner protest fought it in time, and no faith in basic values gave it a counter balance. It is only from Russia that the vitality and spiritual warmth of feeling the world most needs will come." He tried to prove his point by quoting from *The Mission of the East* by Schubart, a book published in Switzerland two years before, that had been widely read and secretly discussed. It predicted that Russia would save the world from stagnation by the primitive strength and the mysticism of its people who were certain eventually to discard Communism.

The Hungarian hotly contradicted these theories: "You are confusing men and principles," he countered. "No private good will or belief in justice and liberty are effective against party domination enforced by secret police."

A Bulgarian diplomat who was brooding apart from the others suddenly exclaimed with emotion: "If only, oh if only I could obtain a sentence of life imprisonment."

We made him explain. It seemed that if he were captured by the Russians and, on being delivered to his countrymen, sent to prison instead of being executed on the spot, his mother-in-law who had Communist friends, would be able to free him at the first chance of amnesty—but as it was, he preferred going into hiding near the Danish border. Everyone present but ourselves had planned to travel westwards in the next few days, like leaves blown by a strong wind.

Freddy complained of our guests after they had left, for he was disturbed at having been forced to listen to these unpleasant discussions, symptoms of a hopeless situation against which he was powerless.

Letters arrived from friends in western Germany warning us in a roundabout way that they believed Kerzendorf was sure to become a battleground. They advised us to leave at once, to lose no time in coming to stay with them. They advised us to buy horses from peasants, harness them to a cart filled with all it would hold and take flight. The inhabitants of the Eastern provinces had saved more of their possessions by leaving in time than others had by remaining in houses later burned over their heads in warfare. These earnest injunctions gave me a growing wish to abandon everything for safety's sake, instead of submitting passively to events.

But my husband would hear none of it. "I would not be a refugee in other peoples' houses for all the security in the world," he said violently. "We are responsible for our home, we must use our intelligence and courage to keep it. I would rather be killed surrounded by the objects I spent a lifetime collecting than run away like a coward to save my bare existence." I was in an agony of apprehension and feared the worst, but even the constant air raids, often several in one night, did not make him change his mind. Again and again we gathered in the little cellar and yet, each time we walked back under clouds and stars when the planes had ceased their work, happiness overwhelmed me at finding that the enormous, impersonally stupid missiles had miraculously failed to smash our rooms. A breeze in the branches in front of my window brought a rustling sigh of content, for explosions and the deafening noises had blown over, turning the pure air into a gift, like a lease granted anew.

It was worthwhile to be afraid if only to appreciate afterwards with conviction those things for which we were taking the risk, yet was it not irrational to give way to the instinct that made us remain here? My doubts were accentuated by the continual stream of unhappy and dazed refugees, driven forward like cattle.

"Is this why my three sons died in the war?" a woman asked me bitterly.

But the war that should have been abandoned months ago continued with its clumsy waste, young men died, the ailing and aged were drafted indiscriminately, boys of fifteen were sent into the Air Force and often killed. One morning the tragic news of the destruction of Dresden reached us. Had fighting been stopped in time, many lives and this lovely city would have been spared, as well as flourishing towns in the Rhineland, that were reduced to ashes one after another.

Our poor little horse had been requisitioned, so when I wished to visit our neighbours in Lowen again, I walked over on foot. As I entered the usually quietly dignified house I found it in a turmoil. The owner's daughter Hilda, her husband and the young engaged girl had arrived from Silesia the day before. There was now no longer any question of celebrating a marriage on their estate in that province. They had realized the urgency of flight so that they could bring nothing away but small suit-cases in their car. Hilda, her husband and daughter had got up from tea in the library, where first editions and fine manuscripts remained on the shelves, and gone out through the warm rooms filled with beautiful furniture, down passages where cupboards contained silver and linen. When they drove off, the house's familiar aspect with its lighted windows shining peacefully in the dusk made it seem as if the family were going off for a week-end. It seemed a crazy delusion that they were about to leave home never to return.

"Why did my husband and brother refuse to admit this could happen?" Hilda said reproachfully. "I believed them implicitly. We might easily have taken our things away in time."

56

All defence was expected to collapse in the next few days, so that Lowen seemed unsafe to its owners. But perhaps the Western Allies and not the Russians would capture the capital after all, or a fight between the latter and the Anglo-Saxons might break out, in which the German Army could fight the East together with the West? So they conjectured in low voices, nervous of being overheard by their Ukrainian servant who was listening at the door. She was a very pretty and intelligent, fair-haired girl named Pasha, who dressed in a national costume she had brought with her. She came from a well-off peasant family. She was not Communist, she curtsied charmingly when she was spoken to and ran the large household with honesty and efficiency. "What are her feelings towards the advancing Russians? Is she loyal to them or to you?" I questioned the owners of Lowen.

"She is engaged to the young Polish coachman," my hostess answered. "Both of them are unaware of what is happening," she added.

Throughout our conversation the old lady and her family were sorting things out, packing them into suit-cases, and making preparations for sudden flight. During the afternoon their relations and friends continuously passed through on motor-cycles, in cars, in carriages drawn by horses. They stopped at Lowen to ask for a short rest, a drink, a little food, then to disappear again into the night. They were landowners, deserting officers, all as panic-stricken as hunted foxes.

The doorbell rang furiously and an officer in a black SS uniform burst in, accompanied by his wife, a cousin of the hostess, carrying a baby in her arms. His brutal face wore a frightened expression, and as he spoke in terms of hatred against the German Army, the other men's anger and their dislike of the SS was so violently aroused that a quarrel began. But he had to leave immediately: "I must hide, or they will kill me," he said with a sly and terrified look.

An air raid began before I could leave for home and no sooner

57

was it over than another started. We spent a great part of the night in the vaults underground, while the house shook to its ancient foundations.

It was late at night and we were very tired when we returned upstairs to the quaint old-fashioned drawing-room hung with family portraits, where heavy curtains were drawn before the windows and a large clock ticked on a gleaming mirror. As I was listening to my hosts, an opaque shadow fell on the wall opposite me, covering with emptiness what I had seen clearly a moment before. A nail half hidden by cobwebs stuck out, I felt the cold abandonment of an uninhabited house, I was enveloped by icy air and alone in the room. I was released from the vision, warm light played again on the much ornamented walls and people were close around me.

In the early morning my hostess sent me back in her carriage along the road covered with hard frozen snow. I sat next to Pavlik, the Polish coachman, a small pale-faced man with a pointed nose and intelligent eyes. I asked him: "Are you happy here?" He did not answer, only looked at me suspiciously. When I repeated my question, he blushed. "All that matters to me is to save Pasha's life and mine," he said. "I want her to follow me to Poland, where we wish to marry and to settle down. But will we succeed? The Russian Army is now at X." He mentioned the name we had heard in foreign broadcasts but was kept secret from the German population. "We are in a predicament, for if we run away now, while we belong to the German state, we risk being caught and punished. But we must also be careful not to leave Lowen too late, for if the Russians find us in the house there, they will shoot us for serving Germans, even though we did not come here of our own free will. Pasha and I are alone against the whole world. We can't expect forgiveness from any side and if we are not wary, we will be lost. What importance has it if I like or dislike being in Lowen or if I serve its masters for a few weeks longer? Once I have left it I shall not even remember its name. Night and day Pasha and I live absorbed in the thought of our escape and in the hope of our future life together."

"But how will you know when the right moment to leave has come?" I asked.

"The wireless will tell us," he laughed. "A Russian prisoner in Lowen has secretly constructed an excellent radio. We listen every night."

In Kerzendorf the refugees had left to go west and hundreds of French prisoners, evacuated from camps lying in the territory the Russians were nearing, had taken their place, so that one felt transported to a village in France, where nothing but French was spoken. I cautiously talked to the men, although it was severely forbidden, and found them in excellent spirits, certain of the speedy end of their captivity. On Sunday their Catholic priest had celebrated mass in the little Protestant church, the roof of which had been blown off by bombs. The next day when we woke they had gone on to a new destination.

Momentarily the Russian invasion had come to a halt. We knew it to be only a brief reprieve, but it meant that catastrophe was not immediately imminent. The Nazis took advantage of this lull to declare on the wireless that Roosevelt, Churchill and Eden were expected to make a peace proposal. Fake information was given on purpose to soothe the population which was dangerously tired of suffering and fighting without a gleam of hope. Letters to the men at the front were full of descriptions of bombings and hardships so desperate that they influenced soldiers to give themselves up as prisoners, since they believed it to be a way of helping to end the war. The population looked upon American and British troops as saviours coming to liberate them from the Nazi leaders. For nearly everyone it was now the men mercilessly driving them on who were regarded as the real enemies.

A transformation had taken place in the minds of honest men confronted by the clearly visible ruin of their country which would seem incomprehensible and reprehensible once normal times returned. It was no longer unpatriotic or dishonourable for them to betray military plans, it had become a means of saving Germany, of defending house and home by curbing crazy leadership, and was done in an exalted spirit of civil war against a party which was a deadly peril to their country. Information was passed on by every means, by secret wireless sets, by reports, so that never has an adversary known as much about enemy movements as the Allies did about Germany.

Yet a serious revolt before final defeat was improbable. The Gestapo was on the alert for possible conspiracies, and the Nazi leaders were too closely guarded to be approached by their enemies. Visitors could not see them until they had been searched for weapons, and Hitler and Goering drove in bullet-proof cars and trains.

For one whole day we were able to discuss events with friends who had come out to Kerzendorf, amongst them the landowner whom we had last met at the party for Hans' marriage some weeks earlier. Since then he had left his estate and house in Silesia at the last minute, taking with him the employees he believed to be in danger from the Russians. He drove his car along roads crowded by whole villages taking flight in the bitter cold. People carrying heavy bundles containing their last, most prized possessions threw them down on the roadside to ease their progress. He passed guards driving forward long columns of political prisoners and Jews who were being evacuated from camps. They could scarcely walk from exhaustion, and to his horror he saw a guard shoot men unable to go any further.

Another guest was an officer from the military headquarters in the capital, who had also lost an estate a few days before that had belonged to his family for five hundred years. He had managed to save his furniture and pictures by sending them to Hamburg, but the place that had supported his forbears for centuries had irretrievably gone.

Land generally brings an income incomparably inferior to that derived from finance or industry. But by giving a basic

60

security to man's essential needs for food and fuel, it offers a chance for a family's survival in hard times, provides an unchanging background, against which tradition, beliefs and habits can develop, to be handed down without interruption from generation to generation. Now a gigantic change had taken place in eastern Europe that was of a more far-reaching influence than the French Revolution in 1789, when the social order had been restored a very few years afterwards by Napoleon. In Poland, Czechoslovakia, Hungary and east Germany we were witnessing a more lasting upheaval, for the entire upper class had been swept away, large and small landowners, farmers, the whole middle class and most intellectuals had been eliminated, leaving an indistinct colorless crowd. One day something would emerge from it, but for the moment nothing was visible but the dictates of the state. We were also witnessing defeat in the century-old fight against the Slavs who had been slowly conquered and pushed back East for a thousand years. They were at present surging forward in an overwhelming force, not only to take provinces by military force, but to bring to the West their own conception of government, that of Byzantine power over disarmed and speechless masses.

Both men believed that in contrast to the French landowners at the end of the eighteenth century, they would never be able to retake possession of the places of their birth. Even if it were possible for them to return there, it would be as strangers under unrecognizable conditions. The officer was indignant about the Fuehrer's plan to organize a formation named 'Werewolf', that was to consist of armed civilians ordered to sabotage and impede the enemy in every way once they had invaded the country.

"It is a criminal plan, the fruit of desperation, of no practical value," he complained. He had given a written memorandum to his general, who agreed with him in his efforts to stop these measures.

He told us how a friend of his, Count Schulenburg, former

61

Ambassador to Moscow, had been executed a short time before for conspiring against Hitler, and had been ordered to Ribbentrop's house together with the entire staff of the Foreign Office, to listen to an important speech in which the Foreign Minister disclosed details of the approaching German victory. When the speaker caught Count Schulenburg's eye and noticed his sardonic gleam, there was a moment's pause. Then Ribbentrop broke out, staring at Schulenburg with ill-contained fury: "If National-Socialists are defeated and are forced to go, we shall slam the door with such a crash that the whole globe will resound from it."

The officer warned us of the risk of staying in Kerzendorf. His urgent advice to us was that since my husband did not consent to go West, he should remain where he was, while I, in more acute peril, he believed, than a man, should leave immediately.

Freddy refused to admit the shocking possibilities, and I felt uneasily that he was unprepared for them and at their mercy. Until today he had planned and looked ahead for both of us. Our parts were now suddenly reversed, because I was instinctively less surprised by what seemed inconceivable to him. How could I go off alone in search of safety?

"If Kerzendorf becomes a battlefield before you can get away, you must build a small hut in the meadows on the top of a ditch, store food in it and seek refuge there against gunfire," he added thoughtfully, to my husband's incredulous surprise.

He promised to telephone us reliable news every few days in careful terms: "The patient's health is unchanged, worse or hopeless," were the expressions we agreed on to describe the German defence.

Meanwhile, the officer's beautiful young wife, attractively dressed and much made up, became increasingly bored with the conversation. Since her husband was paying too little attention to her she reached for a book on the library shelf behind her. It was the Almanach de Gotha, one of several volumes containing the names and dates of reigning or former reigning families, another of Counts, one of Barons and the last of untitled nobility. She looked up absorbed. "My favourite book," she said, "the only one I read, for it is an unending source of interest." She turned the pages, voluptuously uttering little exclamations under her breath.

"Oh, darling," she broke into her husband's moving description of the Russian advance in Saxony, "what do you think? Anna is forty-one years old and she only admits to thirty-five." Then, "Did you know Paul's wife was a Kinsky?"

George, another of our guests, was a member of the Foreign Office. He told us that everything had been prepared for officials of his, as well as of all the other ministries to leave Berlin in a few days. He had come to offer to take away any of our possessions in a private car he had chartered with a friend, and to deposit them in a bank in the west for safe keeping. But Freddy absolutely refused to hear of it. "I alone am responsible for my things," he answered in response to my entreaties to accept this offer. According to George, everyone was taking flight from Berlin. The trains were packed. The Duke of Mecklenburg would never have succeeded in leaving without his pretty daughter's ingenuity. She walked along the train her father was longing to enter and, approaching a window out of which soldiers were looking, implored them in a whisper to help her by pretending to arrest her father. The soldiers immediately entered into the spirit of the plot, came out onto the platform and escorted the Duke to a compartment from which they ordered all occupants to leave. They then firmly locked the door and soon they were smoking their so-called prisoner's cigarettes and conversing with him in a friendly way until they had gone as far as the grateful Duke had wished to travel.

My husband sent for Wilhelm, the gamekeeper and gardener of Kerzendorf, to consult with him and his guests about which trees he should cut down to leave more air for some of the old giants, and which bushes he should transplant to bring out the park's design more harmoniously. I fought for the life of each tree, but in the end we marked two beeches and one oak that would have to go.

In discussing next summer from the point of view of plants, we had forgotten our own precarious existence. The feeling of insecurity returned when our guests took leave, for now there was a solemnity about every parting. Unspoken fears for each other and for oneself made every second poignant with the thought that it was perhaps the last time we would see each other, and stamped words and gestures unforgettably on one's mind.

Chapter VI

SHOULD WE stay or should I use all my persuasion to make Freddy leave Kerzendorf?

I went to Berlin one day to find out what other people thought about the question. Destruction there was worse than ever but my mind was closed to all new impressions and I could only think of the problem: To stay? To leave?

Most people seemed to be taking flight. The doctor, Maria Daelen, was leaving Berlin the following day after she had been warned that the Gestapo was collecting evidence against her and that she would be arrested. Diplomats were leaving, the Swiss to Bavaria, the Spaniards to Thuringen. Only one person I knew, Charles, a lawyer, was going to remain with his parents on the outskirts of Berlin.

"The war will be finished long before the enemy arrives at the capital," he believed. And it sounded logical. "The army will capitulate in time to avoid the destruction of Berlin."

I met the wife of a violinist who was on her way to a concert which her husband was giving. She told me that Speer, the Nazi Minister of Defence, had ordered theatrical and musical performances to continue because he believed them to be important for the morale of the population.

She concluded, "I am quite relieved. I just heard from the best source that the Russians and the other Allies have started fighting each other."

She could not have read the bulletins that day, for the military situation was rapidly deteriorating as the Russians had started to move forward again.

Discussions with different people had brought me no nearer

to a decision. Advice was futile because the personal reasons for actions of others were different in each case and could not serve as an example. We had to look to ourselves alone to find a solution.

Next morning, when the loud hooting of a motor-car called us to the window, we saw my sister-in-law Elly and her old maid, both carrying a few small suit-cases, step out of a large truck filled with soldiers. She told us that in the last few days the noise of shooting and fighting had come even closer to Buckow. Her houses had been requisitioned for a Hitler school for young boys instead of for Foreign Office officials. The orders were executed amidst the roar of guns and although everyone concerned knew that children could not be taken there under these circumstances, no one dared protest, as it might have elicited the dangerous word 'defeatism' which was equivalent to treachery. Soldiers leaving in the direction of Kerzendorf had offered to take Elly along, and there she was, holding two little bags that contained all she had been able to take away from her house. The furniture, pictures and everything else associated with her whole life were gone. As yet she did not realize her losses; it was enough at the moment to be safe, to have got away from a perilous spot, but soon she would miss first one thing, then another. She would recall them until each was burnt into her consciousness and became far more real to her by its absence, than it was while in her possession.

She was not happy in Kerzendorf for she felt in danger. The nightly air raids upset her and more still the fear of the Russians' approach. She telephoned and wrote for a car that could take her away. She raised heaven and earth until finally she got in touch with some people who were leaving Berlin in a truck and who promised to pick her up on the way to Salzburg. They were late in arriving at seven in the evening as arranged, and her fear that she might have been forgotten, that she was condemned to risk her life by remaining a little longer in Kerzendorf, was contagious. We waited up with her, listen-

66

ing to her complaints, afraid to utter our own very disturbed thoughts.

It started raining softly, then heavily. The car arrived at last, in the midst of a cloudburst, and we accompanied her to the door. A rough and bad-tempered driver at first refused to let Elly and her maid take their modest luggage. We had to entreat him before he consented to allow them to vanish into the interior of the large vehicle holding on to the suit-cases. A few seconds later the truck was swallowed up by the dark night on its way to safety, while we returned to the house with heavy hearts.

The next time my husband telephoned to his officer friend the answer was, "The patient is slowly weakening."

We expected a Danish journalist for lunch that day who was coming to say farewell to us before leaving Berlin by a train due to arrive at one o'clock. About noon, two or three planes suddenly descended from the sky like hawks before the siren had had time to give its warning. They nearly touched the roof and grazed the tree tops, departing in a deafening roar before we could decide where to take shelter.

Half an hour later our visitor arrived in a state of considerable alarm. While on his way to Kerzendorf the same planes that had troubled us flew only a few yards above the little local train in which he had been travelling and had begun shooting at it with a machine-gun. The locomotive stopped and the terrified passengers ran into the fields on either side and threw themselves down flat between the furrows. When the attack ceased, the Dane re-entered his compartment to find the bags and parcels he had left there stolen, and we mourned for the cheese, sardines and other now precious delicacies he had intended to bring us.

Our friend did not take his experience for granted, but openly and nervously expressed how much he hated it. By this time we had a great distrust of people who accepted the worst catastrophes in sheep-like resignation, not out of self-control or admirable courage, but from weariness, from a lack of reaction. How could there ever be an end to what was passively accepted? During the French Revolution, when aristocrats had died on the scaffold with disdainful equanimity before a more and more indifferent public, it was Madame Du Barry, who sobbed and begged for her life with a total lack of restraint, who moved the spectators to such horrified compassion, the authorities were forced to stop public executions. Our friend showed great emotion over his narrow escape and to hear him speak with undimmed vivacity of the charm of being alive, was a welcome contrast to grand words and unnatural calm.

Although the trip to Kerzendorf had now become dangerous, we had one other visitor, a Swiss member of the Red Cross who was passing through in the course of his duties to look after French and Belgian prisoners of war. In this humanitarian purpose he was continually risking his life and had barely escaped being caught in a bombardment just before his arrival. He not only had Swiss papers with him containing news of military events as yet unknown to us, but to our joy he brought letters and messages from friends from whom we had been cut off.

At a time when we stared anxiously into an unpredictable future, these letters were voices speaking in the dark, bringing comfort that took away our feeling of isolation and drew us back into the warm circle of humanity. When our visitor left in his car, we looked after him as birds in a cage watch another take free flight into the blue sky.

My husband had to go to Berlin for two days and so did Ida, the maid. I was as anxious for their safety in the city as I dreaded an attack in Kerzendorf, where I had remained with only the old cook and Bibi as companions.

In the afternoon Hilda telephoned me from Lowen where I had visited her only the day before, telling me in a tense voice: "Will you please receive Alfred tomorrow morning at six o'clock? Does it suit you? Answer yes or no."

Alfred was a young count, twenty-two years old, who had

owned one of the largest estates in East Prussia until three weeks previously. He was an only son of a father long dead, whose mother had brought him up to fit him for his inheritance of a great fortune and his responsibilities for the welfare of many people. She had believed in the future of National-Socialism, had been intimate with Nazi politicians, in her one-track opportunism became a party member and talked Alfred into following her example. It did not trouble her that in so doing she had antagonized the other East Prussian landowners who, with rare exceptions, were in opposition to the government.

Alfred was a cultured young man, spoke several languages, and had grown up among beautiful inherited collections. He was not sent to school but was taught by a tutor. He had visited mostly museums and churches on his travels and had met few people outside those in his own province. Crowds were odious to him and he remembered with disgust the unpleasant occasions when he had been forced to enter a full train or bus. His tall slender figure, his movements, his manner of speech were of a natural distinction, an unconscious elegance. He was straight-forward and sincere, but afflicted with a serious defect: he had no judgment. By nature he was repelled by cruelty, easily shocked by any vulgarity. How then could he have joined National-Socialism and consorted with its representatives? It was because, like some royalty, he had no sense of discrimination and believed everybody but his peers in birth to be of a different and inferior race. At the same time he obscurely thought that ugliness in looks, the loud ostentation that grated irritatingly on his nerves, were identical with the Voice of the People. In his eyes they impersonated the magic of success, the result of grasping and pushing of which he knew himself incapable and which he naively envied as a symbol of strength. Ruthlessness, though foreign to his nature, so impressed him that it made him shy of asserting the Christian principles which were the basis of his education and he was proud of overcoming a spontaneous repulsion which he fought like a prejudice.

69

Alfred had now taken a temporary refuge at Lowen where I had met him the other day. I was surprised at Hilda's sending him to me at such an unusual hour, but her tone was insistent and we had learned to ask no questions on the telephone. A German expression defines the quality of a relationship: "A person ready to steal horses with you." It is the essence of friendship, to help the other without discussion in any emergency, good or bad, in fun or in earnest. Hilda was a friend, so I answered "Yes" without knowing to what I assented, as I would have expected her to do had I put the question to her.

The cook woke me on the radiant spring morning and we prepared breakfast. Alfred arrived in a little car packed to the top with luggage. He explained that the military news was so bad that Hilda, her husband and daughter had decided to leave Lowen on that very day, and to make their departure from Lowen as inconspicuous as possible, they had chosen Kerzendorf as a rallying point, where they were all due to arrive at a different hour during the morning and then drive off together. Alfred had come in advance to persuade me to accompany them, either with or without Freddy, to give me time to pack and to give Alfred an opportunity to convince me of the necessity of taking flight. But how could I possibly leave without consulting my husband who was absent and whom I could not reach? The well-meant advice served only to unsettle me.

The others seemed to have been delayed, for it was already eight o'clock, then nine, and still they had not come. Suddenly the siren blew its weird whistle. Running to the window I saw small specks of silver and white very high up in the dazzling blue sky, and more and still more coming. I hastened to the shelter, while Alfred chose to stay in the house. There were nothing but planes in the world, clouds of them like mosquitoes arriving in formation from all sides, quadrilles meeting and mingling in changing geometrical patterns. Round white puffs of smoke, as if from toy guns, stood stiffly around them, small mushrooms were thrown out and slowly floated earthwards.

70

For a moment all the glitter and throbbing seemed an eternal fixture. It had taken over all movement, all liberty. We were condemned to idleness, watching motionlessly, prepared for fatal accidents. At last the steel birds assembled, lines, triangles, quadrangles were blown together, gathered and left the horizon in one majestic stream. A blackbird sang and called to another who replied with the sweetness of a flute. They also had been frightened, reviving after having been silenced by too large rivals, and slowly an order we knew had been torn apart closed around us again.

When I came back to the house still shaken, I found Alfred pale, but he only said, "Let us walk." We went through the park in which every bush, every branch was covered with the first green of the year. The earth was brown and soft to walk on, a few violets showed their heads in the grass. In this early season, when the trees were not yet covered with leaves, the design in which they had been planted came out with great purity. How could I leave all this of which I was a part?

Alfred began talking of his garden, of roses he had pruned last year, of a half-completed swimming pool. Could he seriously believe that he would ever be able to return to the province which the Russians had seized? He spoke of what had gone as though it were still his and of the past as though it was the present. I did not interrupt him but let him continue a dream that would end soon enough. While listening I struggled with my own reality, trying to catch hold of my own present, to cling to what was about me, to my wishes and to my hopes.

We heard the hooting of motor horns and went towards them. Hilda and her family got out of one car, their friends from another. They came into the library having extracted a magnum bottle of brandy from under their suit-cases, the only one they had saved from their house in Silesia. We drank and all talked at the same time in growing excitement at the danger of staying, the necessity of leaving, knowing it to be a critical occasion, a final event.

71

"My mother is leaving in a cart in the next few days," said Hilda to me. "She will ring you up before she goes. By then you can have discussed the matter with Freddy and can give her an answer. It is your last chance to get away, I fear. Now we must drive off, we are late."

There was a stir, all got up. Hilda drank to our meeting again in the near future. There were embraces, last injunctions, messages to my husband. A few seconds later the room was silent and empty but for some half-emptied glasses.

When my husband arrived from the capital he was exhausted and visibly happy to be back in the country. Before I could tell him of their advice and proposals, he interrupted me, determined not to hear what he knew I was going to say, and obstinately resolved to continue a personal life in which he could express himself. He said reprovingly: "I do not like the way you have arranged the vases. A few forsythia branches in each room are quite enough, more spoil the effect and divert the attention from the decoration and furniture. It is in as bad taste as a woman who wears too many jewels." He then arranged the flowers himself in a very effective way.

"I hope you used the right glasses. What drinks did you give them?" He was relieved to find I had made no mistakes. Then he talked of people he had met that day, and of an Augsburg silver ink-stand he had been tempted to buy. It was impossible to make him listen to my doubts, to suggest packing, to tell him of Hilda's mother's idea to take him and me, or me alone, to safety. Whenever I started to explain, another air raid drove us out. There were almost ceaseless attacks now, three or four during that evening.

As it was one of the days when electricity was cut off we lit a fire to read by its light and decided to sort out old letters of Freddy's that filled a large trunk he had not looked into for years. He read some sentences aloud to me, then gave them to the flames which twisted them and darkened the sheets to a deep brown until they finally dissolved into light-grey flakes. A big

72

parcel of letters was from his parents, touching for their pride in him, others were from him to them as a young man, their only son. They reminded him of his ambitions, his plans, of his difficult and numerous examinations, of his gambling debts. He was desperately remorseful about them and grateful when they generously complied with his requests. The worries of that time seemed to weigh lightly in comparison with today's questions of life and death.

"The period before 1914 seems happier in retrospect than it was," declared Freddy. "It is true that the material side of life was easier, currencies safe, passports for travelling unheard of, but as we knew nothing of future tragedy we were unaware of our luck. A high price had to be paid for security, for conventions were rigid and stood out unchallenged. Any infraction against them brought social ostracism, especially in Central Europe where narrow standards of behaviour had been dictated by the Court, the regiments and a bourgeois Victorian society. They formed a pattern so delicate that continual care alone could save one from disaster. I believe that it is the years 1919 to 1929 that will remain in people's memory as a short but unique period of comparative liberty from society as much as from the state."

We went on talking about past problems until I realized, waking up in the middle of the night, that I had not told my husband about the almost unanimous advice given to us, and that I absolutely had to make him listen to me; perhaps I should write him a letter? This was my last thought before I went to sleep.

The first sound I heard in the morning was the telephone ringing. Could it be the owner of Lowen putting the fatal question? But it was a call for Freddy. From where I stood I could hear the voice of his friend, the officer, clearly enunciating the words, "The patient's health is failing, he can only live a few days longer. I am going off by plane in a few hours, my wife is accompanying me. Good luck to you. May we see each other again." My husband put down the receiver. Then he lifted his eyes and looked at me. For a moment neither of us moved or spoke. "Hilda's mother will soon be leaving too," I got out with difficulty. "What shall I say to her when she telephones?"

Freddy gave me a surprised glance. "Everyone has to make his own decisions," he said absent-mindedly. He walked to the window, opened it, bent out and smiled. I followed his eyes. Outside Bibi was barking at a large goose which had strayed onto the lawn, but at the same time backing nervously towards the house as she was afraid of the bird's venomous hissing. A strong April sun made everything blindingly alive, reflected even in the bark of the trees bursting with sap, and shone on the lake's mirror-like surface gleaming at the end of the straight alley.

Looking in front of him, Freddy said quietly, "We love it, we must defend it."

Before I could say a word he turned around and began to rearrange his room in a leisurely way. He moved a table, a chair, took two statuettes from his desk and placed them on the mantelpiece.

"This is a great improvement, don't you think? How could I not have thought of it before?"

At that moment the telephone rang again. I went slowly to answer it. "Are you coming with me?" It was the voice of the owner of Lowen. "You can bring one suit-case, small enough to carry yourself. There is space for no more in the cart. I owe it to your mother to say, 'Come.' If you don't you put yourself at the mercy of anybody or anything."

I did not hesitate, but said very smoothly, "Thank you very much, I shall stay here."

"Good luck," was the answer, and after a pause the same ominous words as those of Freddy's friend. "Hope to see you again."

After this conversation a weight was lifted from my mind. Now I had joined Freddy in an irrevocable decision by consciously refusing my last chance of leaving Kerzendorf, the monotonous argument and doubts had fallen to the ground. I no longer hesitated; I had chosen. We were both united in the same purpose, in the same wish to defend our home and were ready to accept the consequences, whatever they might be.

Chapter VII

WE WENT on with the routine of daily existence as though it would continue for ever. Having always been surrounded by many people, friends and acquaintances had now vanished, carried off by an instinct of self-preservation, and we were left behind together to face the approaching invasion as people in a shipwreck cling to their ship. To be alone in the midst of silence and leisure was a new experience in which our conversation, discussions about books and the care of garden and woods were absorbing sources of pleasure. We were all the more conscious of our enjoyment knowing well the sinister reasons that had brought it about, and regarded every fragile moment of happiness as a precious gift.

We never mentioned to each other the enormous fact constantly at the back of our minds, that the Russian Army was only an hour's march away. Everything was turning out far worse than we had feared. Until a short time ago it seemed probable that American and British troops would join the Russians in conquering the capital, or that an armistice would be concluded before the fighting reached Berlin. But now that hope was dead. The truism, "Things never turn out either as well or as badly as one expects," proved false, as events continued to develop before our eyes far beyond the limits of what we had imagined.

Electricity had been cut off in our and all the neighbouring villages, although it had been retained at the Daimler motor-works in Ludwigsfelde, despite the fact that the factory was no longer able to work. Orders had been given a week previously to save the machinery from capture by the Russians by dismantling it and sending it west, but no one dared to admit that transport had become impossible since the railway system had completely broken down. When, a few days later, the parts were brought back to the plant and the workers solemnly ordered to reinstall them, the plans had meanwhile been destroyed to save them from falling into enemy hands. The equipment was left lying on the ground, while Belgians, Yugoslavs and other workers strolled about aimlessly. Since some of them had secretly constructed wireless sets, rumours originating in these news broadcasts spread in terrified whispers, passed on from mouth to mouth.

One day in the middle of April 1945 a man arrived breathless at our house, as perturbed as a messenger in Greek tragedy, to report that the town of Luckenwald, twenty-five miles away, was on fire and that enemy tanks were approaching Kerzendorf. With him were peasants of our village, accompanied by their wives and by girls in tears, who came to my husband to seek his advice. Should they stay and hide, or leave? They would follow whatever example we set them. Until now they had been so strongly influenced by propaganda and by the menace of punishment for the smallest sign of defeatism, that it was the first time any of them had dared face the truth that the war was lost and its conclusion was drawing near. It was too late for them to go away for we were surrounded by fighting on all sides. Freddy attempted to quieten their panic by telling them that he firmly believed that the tales of the Russian raping of women were nothing but propaganda.

The seven Serb prisoners who had been allotted to Kerzendorf by the government to do the farmwork in place of men away at the war, accompanied them to talk over the situation. They were homesick for their families and for their own country where they owned large farms, but they waited the end of the war with philosophical patience. They were warmly dressed in clothes distributed by the Red Cross, but as my husband had found their food rations insufficient, he had arranged for them to have extra meals at his expense at the village inn during their

77

stay at Kerzendorf, and had seen to it that they were well looked after. The eldest one, a tall, grave man with a heavy drooping moustache, told Freddy that we should consider them as friends willing to help us in any emergency, or to act as interpreters since they all spoke fluent Russian. He had brought a letter written in Russian in which he stated that Freddy had behaved like a brother to them, and together with my husband they nailed this curious certificate on the front door.

A little later our old chauffeur, Monk, who lived with his wife in a small house next door to us, arrived unexpectedly. Some months before he had been enrolled in the Volkssturm, a military unit composed of the older, less physically fit men who had been rejected for military service at the beginning of the war. The officers and men of his regiment had fled from the Russians, discarded their uniforms, thrown away their arms, and like himself had disbanded and made for home before they were taken prisoner.

I had a private consultation with Ida, my maid, who was a passionate connoisseur of house linen and had presided over my parents' linen and our own for so many years that she considered it as much her property as ours. We were firm allies in our joint determination to save the material objects we believed to be essential to life, so we set out to hide what we were anxious to keep, as had innumerable women faced by the same type of situation throughout history. We piled clothes, carpets and linen into a large closet in a corner of Ida's room and pushed a large cupboard in front of it. Then we packed trinkets into a tin box, amongst them a wrist-watch, my brother's last gift to me before he died, and Ida's that was a present from a man she had been engaged to, both wrapped in opaque golden-colored paper to protect them from damp. My husband refused to part with his watch. "I hold on to the only thing still working in a disrupted world," he said.

Concealing a spade under my arm, I took Ida into the park, along the avenue of trees that shed big rain-drops on our hair, over to the little lake lying in a hollow invisible from the house where as a child I had believed that Narcissus had gazed in rapture at his own image in the smooth surface of the water. There was no noise except a branch snapping in the undergrowth, and once a bird cried out a warning. The calm remoteness surrounding us was in heartrending contrast to the thought of the nearby battle. We nervously searched for the best spot to bury our treasures and dug a hole deep into the soft sweet-scented soil at the foot of a majestic beech tree, where I remembered having once lain for hours to seek refuge from a scolding. After covering the ground with twigs and leaves to make it seem undisturbed, we impressed the scene on our memory so that we should recognize it again, and carefully counted bushes and trees before walking home with the secret shared between us. We felt more reassured against the future for having taken these few feminine precautions against impending disaster.

The storm had already overtaken us, for every few seconds we were startled by flashes of lightning on the horizon, while the sound of machine-guns came unmistakably clear to our ears and observer planes roared backwards and forwards directly over our roofs. When my husband got a call through to the city he learned that the siege of Berlin had begun and that the heavy shooting we heard was that of an artillery attack on the city.

Night came, bringing only a short respite, for at midnight we were awakened by a wailing of the siren that blew on and on as if it had lost its head, while we clumsily tried to get into our clothes by the uncertain light of a candle.

Ida arrived accompanied by the dignified old wife of the most important peasant on the farm, who was so nervous she could hardly speak, and by pretty Mrs. Zarn, the wife of Rudolph, our servant, who was away fighting on the Eastern Front. She and her two daughters, Ulla and Inge, as well as a refugee couple, Mr. and Mrs. Fest, and their daughter, shared the rooms on one side of our house.

"Russian tanks are on the road approaching Kerzendorf,"

they told us in terror. This was the explanation of the siren's prolonged warning.

We went out of doors with them and stood watching the shadows flitting about in the night. A man who had gone off to the village to find out what was happening returned with the news that half an hour previously Russian tanks had nearly reached Kerzendorf, then unexpectedly turned back to where they had come from. The siren stopped, but, we thought wearily, it would soon start again, to announce fresh dangers and drive us back into the cold night. We threw ourselves on to our beds without undressing to get a little rest, tensely expecting to be called at any minute, but to our surprise we were not disturbed again that night.

We got up early the next day to the sound of shooting, the heavy bass of artillery, the light and more regular tapping of machine-guns. Silver and white planes buzzed high up in the sky, others roared just above our heads and darted down to shoot at trucks, cars or passengers on the roads, which had now become impassable. We congregated in the little air-raid shelter, and for a while silently huddled together in the musty darkness, women and men both equally frightened. I derived comfort from Bibi, who was sleeping peacefully in my arms, full of confidence in my power to protect her. She and I lived in universes of separate motives and reactions, yet we were deeply united by our knowledge of each other.

The sun outside was hot, a spring sun that brought out the buds and flowers. Though it was dangerous to go out into the open, I quickly slipped over to the house and got some books and chairs. I placed them just outside the entrance to the shelter. For a long time we looked at illustrations in a work on eighteenth-century French pavilions, known as 'Follies'. Freddy became so entranced with one of those buildings that he decided he must have a small tea-house in Chinese style, the roof turning up at the sides like slanting Mongol eyes, built at the end of the park. He could not decide what sort of silver and china would be best for serving meals there, although it must be eighteenth century of course, of a simple, rustic design. The china we would use was a set of Dresden porcelain of around 1730, decorated with Chinese motifs painted in mauve, red and gold by Herold.

"Perhaps," he corrected himself musingly, "that pattern would be rather too elaborate for an open-air summer house. Another set of Dresden china, painted with butterflies in a severe, stylized design, might be better."

I was worried about the risk of their being broken on the way over to the pavilion, but this made my husband extremely angry.

"We must be very careful in taking them out, but I implore you not to fall into the petty bourgeois error of not using precious things. Everything you touch, everything that is in daily use, should be as attractive as possible. The next thing you'll suggest is that we should shut up the drawing-room except for parties and put slip covers on the chairs."

He got up to try to telephone to his carpenter and discuss the building of the pavilion, when we were interrupted by a terrific explosion followed by a blast that threw us violently against the wall of the shelter. Before we could pick ourselves up there was another and still another upheaval, then silence. Retreating German troops had blown up a railway bridge, Wilhelm the gardener told us later; a house had collapsed under the explosion, and windows in the village and most of our own were shattered.

We settled down again to wait for hours, until far into the afternoon, while the gunfire drew nearer, and we heard the rolling of wheels on the road nearby.

While we waited we talked once more about architecture, and discussed how we could improve the haphazard design of our house.

"We must change the front door and the line of the roof, and pull down the shabby wooden veranda," said Freddy. "We will grow vines, ivy and rambling roses to cover the crevices of the bombed house, to make it look like one of those romantic ruins that were erected artificially a hundred and fifty years ago. Then," he continued, "as soon as it is feasible, we will go off on a holiday to Lisbon." We had once lived in Portugal for a long period. "Soon it may be possible to travel there by boat."

To be in peace for a while in a country where, as in Portugal, there still flourished a wise old civilization, where buildings had pink or turquoise colored walls and flowers, where fruit blossomed all year round, and to see friends again from whom we were separated by this nightmare, gave us a new will to live. Freddy went on talking to the accompaniment of heavy shooting, continuing to plan and gaze into the future.

A sudden shot from a plane overhead brought us back to the present. Voices called out and two or three men came running up to us almost incapable of speaking in their excitement. They brought unexpected and wonderful news: a white flag of truce had just been hoisted from our church by the inhabitants who had driven away some reckless men who had wanted to try to defend the village. The Russian troops had taken the Dresden–Berlin Autostrada that by-passed our village and were leaving Kerzendorf in their rear. Had a battle taken place, we were certain to have been caught in it and killed, so although we knew our troubles were far from over, we were intensely grateful to have escaped immediate peril.

Once back in the house, it was not only a relief to eat because we were hungry, but the business of getting a meal ready to the booming accompaniment of artillery was a reassuringly normal pursuit in the midst of bewildering circumstances.

When we tried the telephone, it was as dead as the now silent radio. We found ourselves cut off from the elusive news on which our personal fate depended. Our severance from the rest of the world was complete; we were now limited to our own personal experience.

There was a loud hammering on the door, which echoed

through the house. When my husband opened the door, a tall, fair-haired officer in a uniform we recognized as Russian although we had as yet never seen one, stood on the doorstep. It was the conqueror present in flesh and blood. When he entered the room, the Russian Army itself was in our home, taking possession. As always, reality differed from anticipation, for it was not he who was violent, but Bibi who flew at his legs before we could stop her, while the soldier made a friendly gesture towards the outraged little dog. Noticing the Serb's letter, he read it, solemnly nodded his head and told a Pole who was accompanying him as an interpreter, to tell us not to be alarmed. He talked in the serious tones of a kindly grown-up soothing frightened children, and helpless though we were, we had a mutual respect for each other's unalterable position.

He stalked through the rooms in a formal search for German deserters. Then, his duty done, he gravely saluted with great dignity and departed, leaving us speechless and trembling.

The refugees and Ida all decided to spend the night together in the Zarns' living-room and stay awake. Freddy undressed and went to bed as usual, while I shut the door on my silent room and waited with beating pulse. A candle fitfully lit the light grey walls and curtains, the books bound in red leather, and the brilliant red shawl in my grandmother's portrait. I thought of her happy and sheltered life, and of her good fortune in having died in 1913 just before the war. That her grand-daughter should find herself at the mercy of Russian soldiers would have been beyond the limits of her imagination.

It was half-past one at night when, between gusts of wind, I heard heavy knocks on the front door. I started up. Should I hide in the garden? But what if they searched for me and discovered me there? I woke my husband who was sound asleep, and ran rapidly to the sitting-room in the other part of the house where the six women and Mr. Fest, the refugee, were gathered, leaving Freddy to go to the door. We heard the sound of two hoarse voices. One seemed drunk, angrily arguing with

83

my husband. A short young soldier burst into the room, sway-ing slightly, accompanied by a Ukrainian who had shown him the way to our house. The soldier roughly sent his companion away, and whipping a revolver out of his pocket, pointed it at Mr. Fest, ordered him out of the room in fluent German, de-claring that he wished to have no man other than himself pre-sent. He sat down on the table, and seemed to take a drunken pleasure in terrifying the half-dozen frightened women in front of him. He suspiciously asked Mrs. Zarn where her husband was, then turning to Ida who happened to occupy the chair nearest to him, ordered her to get up and follow him into the bedroom next door. Before we could intervene, she flew into a passion of rage and edging away from him, told him that she was not going to be touched by a Russian soldier whom she despised and considered inferior to herself, having in the past refused herself to many other much more attractive men. When he had recovered from his surprise he got up, waved his gun and aimed uncertainly at her. She kept dodging him, and abused him in a German of which he could not have understood the rude expressions, until a shot went off that luckily only pierced the back of a chair and went into the wall.

We implored his mercy, and Mrs. Zarn's pretty elder daughter Ulla interposed herself between Ida and the soldier. His fancy shifted to her and while Ida stood still for a moment panting, he pointed his gun at the girl and ordered her to follow him. All of us, including Ulla's mother and sister, pleaded in vain. He brutally pulled her into the refugees' room next door, where his Ukrainian companion was busy stealing their clothes. We waited, petrified. After a while the girl called out to her sobbing mother. She went in to her and found the soldier gone.

When we returned to the library, my husband had dis-appeared. Fest came back from the garden where he had hidden after the soldier had taken his and Freddy's watches at the point of a pistol. Stories of the Russian revolution raced through my mind, as the sound of shooting reached us from outside. Was the fact that he was a landowner, a former diplomat, a reason for them to have taken him away? I tried to imagine what had happened and decided to wait for daybreak before starting a search for him.

The ensuing silence was interrupted by an odd noise. We listened attentively. It seemed to be the sound of someone restlessly pacing to and fro in the cook's empty room just above us. Could a Russian be there watching us? None of us dared to investigate, but waited in terror until at last a grey dawn broke through and I ventured out to call Monk and ask him to go upstairs with me. When he had bravely opened the door of the small attic room, we found my husband in an agony of despair. After the Russian had prevented him from coming to help us by driving him upstairs at the point of his pistol and locking him in, he had passed through hours of intolerable humiliation, hearing voices raised in anguish, and being powerless to protect his wife and the other women who were only a few feet away from him. We were witnessing the logical conclusions of defeat. It was the rape of the Sabines all over again, a repetition of the wars of Rome and Greece and ancient Asiatic feuds. It was the symbol of defeat that men should no longer be able to defend their women, to suffer the shame of seeing them become part of the conquerors' loot.

What had happened at our house was typical of what occurred at all others. Villagers and peasants next morning brought the same tale of rape and theft. Our village had been fortunate, for in neighbouring villages many civilians had been killed in skirmishes.

Later on, after knocking at our door, Russian soldiers forced their way in, in spite of the Serb letter. They were not interested in us, but only in our drawers and cupboards which they opened to take out whatever attracted them. One put on my sun glasses, another took a sweater, a third stuffed a vase into his pocket so roughly that it broke, and then threw the pieces out of the window.

85

Half an hour later one of the Serbs, who was standing outside the house, came in to warn me to escape at once. Drunken soldiers were on their way to the house, clamouring for women. I had no time to go to the garden where the others had disappeared, so I went upstairs to the attic and climbed up underneath the roof on a ladder which the Serb then pulled away. He just had time to go downstairs again when from my hiding-place I heard the heavy tread of men. They searched all through the house, and stood for a long ten minutes immediately underneath where I was hiding, cursing angrily at not finding any women.

After a long time I ventured out again and found the farmyard crowded with German soldiers who had deserted their units and were arriving from all directions. They were only half dressed, because they had thrown away the jackets of their uniforms and were looking for civilian clothes to avoid being taken prisoner. We fed them, gave them what we could, and they went on. They brought contradictory reports of what was happening. It seemed that German resistance in front of Berlin had stiffened, and that the Russians might be forced to retreat. If that was so, Kerzendorf might yet become a battlefield. A wave of panic seized the village, and many of its inhabitants began to flee with their carts.

I lost my nerve and ran to Freddy, whom I found calmly sitting in his room studying a map, and begged him to leave at once. He explained to me, trying to soothe me, how we could now not possibly get through to the American troops, and that there was nothing to do but wait where we were.

In the afternoon our clergyman, an intelligent young man, came over from a neighbouring village where he lived with his wife and small son. He came at the risk of his life to see how the inhabitants of Kerzendorf were faring. The night before he had protected his wife by firmly tucking her into bed and lying on top of her while his room was being searched.

When night began to fall, I discussed with Freddy where we should hide and sleep, for soldiers stalking into the house at

86

night could easily catch us unawares. The three Zarns, the refugee woman and her daughter, Ida, and I decided to sleep on the straw in one of the barns, and two of the peasant wives and the Ukrainian refugee with her two little girls and several others resolved to join us there. The Ukrainian was a warm-hearted, motherly woman who spoke fluent Russian, and during the last two days had negotiated between us and the Russians ceaselessly trying to pacify, help and explain. We had another protector in the person of her unusually handsome and gifted son of fifteen, whom we had named Gabriel after a picture of the angel by Raphael. He read what books he could get, wrote poetry, spoke Russian and German, and expressed himself in a way far beyond his age and education. He had been told by his mother to keep watch in front of our barn, hold the soldiers off, and if they insisted on opening the barn, warn us in time for us to escape by a back door leading into the fields. One by one, so as not to attract attention, we very quietly went to our hiding-place. An entire camp of women refugees from the Black Sea had just arrived, people of German origin who had not been in Germany for generations, on their way to they did not know where, walking in troops and carrying their few possessions in bundles. They were to spend the night in a barn a few yards from ours.

Each of us had a knife for use against possible aggressors. Mine was a Fabergé paper cutter my mother always used, made of ivory, with handle of mauve and grey enamel containing two small blades as sharp as razors. We settled in the straw wrapped in blankets, but the ceaseless shooting from waves of planes overhead made sleep impossible, except for the two men who had come to Kerzendorf to see us and had also chosen to spend the night in the barn. They both immediately started to snore. I did not know such snoring existed. Surely the entire village, the whole Russian Army, would hear them; we would be betrayed and lost. When we had woken them up with great difficulty and explained our fears, they were contrite, and promised to do their best not to snore any more, but in two minutes they began again and we were forced to take turns to prod them into wakefulness.

In the middle of the night we were startled by a violent banging and kicking on the doors. With pounding hearts we listened to vociferations in Russian, to the drunken shouting of many voices answered by Gabriel's melodious quiet tones. When they threw themselves against the doors, rattling at the strong bolts, we waded through straw to get to the back door. We found that planks were nailed across it and thought ourselves lost. But the angry voices calmed down, and we heard hoarse laughter.

"Gabriel is leading them away," whispered his mother, as the group besieging us left. Immediately afterwards women's screams and cries for help, which we could explain only too well, came from the nearby barn.

For many hours, we watched the doors and at intervals woke up the snorers, until at about five in the morning all hell broke loose in an appalling bombardment. What house, street or human being could possibly survive it? Through the cracks in the wooden planking we could see the sky light up every few seconds by a lurid yellow and green flash of light. Towards morning the barn grew cold and damp and we all felt sick from fear and sleeplessness. At last morning dawned, and we slipped out to find and question Gabriel.

Several groups of soldiers had come along asking him in Russian, which he could speak, if there were any women behind the door he was guarding. He always managed to put them off, until a whole truck-full of officers arrived. Like all the others before them they first made sure that Gabriel, who had a very feminine type of beauty, was really a boy and every time they were disappointed at finding he was. They made him swear that there were no women in the barn and threatened that if they found he was lying, he would be shot on the spot.

We were trying to cross over to the house unnoticed when new Russian troops came into the farmyard in great numbers.

We all fled into one of the barns, and found ourselves together with French, Polish and village women. Again we hid in the straw trying by all possible means to avoid attracting their attention. One old woman was sitting far back, leaning hidden against a wall, while next to her the young wife of a peasant was crying out hysterically that she could bear it no longer, and wished to die. To our surprise, the old woman laughed and said: "Try to get away from them, by all means, but if they do catch you just shut your eyes and pretend that it is your husband. How often does he fail to ask you if you want his love and force you to it when you do not want it? If you think of it in that way, you will be able to stand it and it will be over quickly." We could hardly hear the end of her words, for a quarrel had started outside between the Russians and the men at the door, until some orders were given in rough tones and the soldiers went away.

Back at the house I found my husband breakfasting, and noticed a new round hole in the window behind him. A few minutes earlier a soldier had climbed onto the sill from the outside, had knocked on the pane and shouted that he wanted a watch. Without waiting for an answer he had fired a bullet that lodged near a mirror. He had then disappeared like a ghost.

I cut short the story of our night adventures in order not to aggravate Freddy's distress at the role of passive bystander that was forced upon him, while I had been obliged to protect myself without his help.

In the next hectic few days women turned themselves into wild cats, jumping out of windows, hiding, disappearing and turning up again. Some of us tried to make ourselves as unattractive as possible by rouging the tips of our noses, putting grey powder on our upper lips to look like moustaches, and combing out our hair wildly. It was diverting, like dressing up for a new part, but unfortunately Freddy caught me at it and found it so horrid that I stopped doing it.

Our house was difficult to escape from, for it took a long time to get from my room to the other side of the building where

I was obliged to climb through the window, on to the trellis work, then down a half broken ladder before I could hide in the park. Our former chauffeur, Monk, and his wife owned a one-storey house quite close. It contained a small unused sitting-room that was comparatively safe, where I brought my books and could sleep on the sofa at night. To reach it I had first to pass through the kitchen and the old couple's bedroom. Even if soldiers did get that far, it was still possible to escape by jumping out of the window. Freddy remained in the house to defend it and visited me from time to time in my retreat. When I was confident that everything was clear, I went over to see him.

One afternoon Gabriel called me out to speak to a number of French officers, soldiers and civilians. They were men and women who had been released from prison camps by the Russians, or had fled from the vicinity of the fighting and bombing and were on their way to the American lines. They warned us that the new Russian troops about to come through to replace the first, said to be an élite, would be even less disciplined. They were enraged by the Russians' refusal to respect their women. Two of the men offered to take me West, by smuggling me through with their group of women, several of whom were without papers. They considered it madness to remain in Kerzendorf, and the girls joined in trying to convince me. But I could not depart, and I was also convinced peace would soon return. A visible sign of it was that for two days bombs had no longer fallen, and we looked superciliously at the now unused air-raid shelter, where we had recently spent so many hours of the day and night.

"Listen to the machine-guns, don't you realize fighting is approaching Kerzendorf?" they insisted.

Courage suddenly failed me. Would there ever be silence again? I put my hands over my ears.

Chapter VIII

IN THE grey morning a solid row of huge tanks came down the road, approaching in an interminable procession. Our gates were forced back and the monsters entered one after another to the accompaniment of hoarse shouts, until every inch of space was filled by the mud-colored vehicles. An officer, who turned out to be the general's aide, detached himself from the mass of soldiers, came towards the house and asked to see me.

The war, he said, was not yet over. No armistice was in sight. The tanks were to stay in the park at Kerzendorf, hidden by the trees from possible German air attack, to be ready for action in the fighting expected during the next few days. The general and his staff were to be billeted in our house, and the aide had come with orders that we and everyone else living with us should be evacuated within an hour. We might take what we wanted along with us. I looked in despair at our books and pictures, hesitating which to choose, which to abandon, trying to imagine which I would regret the most. Each of them dear to us because of the pleasant memories it aroused.

I ran out to the general who was watching the parking of the tanks in their close ranks. When he turned round and I faced a short, red-faced man whose blazing blue eyes were staring at me, I brought out in some confusion that although I well understood the military necessity of the orders and begged him to use all he needed, I wished to commend some objects to his care which had survived many years and several wars already, and asked him if possible to save them for their own sake. He answered: "Houses have been destroyed all over the Ukraine, where I come from. I have lost all trace of my wife and children,

I know only that they took flight from our village when my parents' house, where I was born, went up in flames. Why should I spare anyone or anything here? Thank Hitler and Ribbentrop for it." As he spoke, the earth was vibrating from the bombardment, and I felt overcome by a feeling of complete helplessness.

But then he continued by telling me of his suffering and how his own unhappiness made him understand my fears. In the midst of the violence of war and in contrast to it, between two people from different parts of the world brought up in surroundings inconceivably dissimilar, a mutual confidence was born, based on a common feeling of sadness at the cruel stupidity of destruction. He took my hand and said: "You must leave, but I give you my word to protect your home."

Having broken to my husband the terrible news of our forced departure—terrible news indeed, because in all probability we would never return to our home, or only to find it devastated—Ida and I hastened to her room, shoved away the heavy cupboard from the hiding-place we were so proud of, quickly took out a few cans of food, and left everything that was not urgently needed concealed where it was. We planned to place our suitcases in a large dogcart and harness it to a horse borrowed from a peasant, but I had small faith in possessions that could easily be torn out of one's hands and believed only in the safety of things either swallowed, buried or wrapped around one's body. It was the end of April. The warm weather was approaching, and as we visualized the discomfort of having nothing but a heavy dress to wear, and no chance of obtaining lighter clothing, the other women, like myself, put on several layers of underwear, a summer dress, two blouses, a skirt over a woollen frock, sweaters on top of each other—in fact everything we considered indispensable for the four seasons. When we looked round at each other, we were as fat as Russian dolls and could hardly move our arms that stood out stiffly from our sides. Over all this I wore a dark brown Chanel coat, which I remember with gratitude, for no evening dress or frock that I have ever possessed has ever given me greater satisfaction. It was neither too heavy nor too light, its cut was as inconspicuous as a man's coat, and it was ideally suited to the very unusual circumstances. The gay autumn morning when I had bought it in Paris seemed as remote as an event in another century.

I fetched a wheelbarrow from a shed and threw the cans into it, but when I decided to bring along some books to divert us during the wearisome hours of waiting, Ida protested sharply, while busily packing two fragile glass vases she had once bought when we were together in Venice. Nothing I said could deter her from taking some large cooking pots and pans. She protested:

"I refuse to start a new household without them."

"But the big ones?" I asked.

To hear her angry comments, we might have been diplomats transferring to a new post with a house to furnish with a complete kitchen outfit, and she insisted on stocking the entire set of pots in the wheelbarrow.

Freddy came along with a long-hoarded bag of coffee, and four hats made by the London hat-maker Lock. He would not part with them, although I pointed out that they seemed unnecessary in rainy woods. "When life becomes normal again, I shall need them as before," he explained. "Besides they are beautiful objects that must not fall into ignorant hands." I was scolded for bringing out some large first editions I particularly cared for, but as I was more pliable than the others, I obediently carried them back to the library. Having hidden the books I most wanted under cans, I covered them with a blanket for Bibi.

Meanwhile the other people who had been evicted had assembled in the farmyard and were busy stacking bundles and bedding on a cart to be drawn by a second horse. Where should we make for? There was shooting on all sides and the peasants wished to avoid the highway where their horses might be requisitioned. We finally decided to go straight for the woods, to a clearing we all knew, where we could settle for a few hours or days until we could either return home or get through to some village. We ran in and out of the house laden with bundles in ant-like absorption, brushing past the swarming soldiers amongst whom were women in uniform. One woman soldier was kind in helping the crying children to climb into a cart and settled them next to their harrassed mother.

At the last moment, my husband had an excellent idea: "Why not take along a couple of straw garden chairs, so that we need not sit on the wet grass? We can put them out in the sun and talk." While they were rapidly fetched and stacked in the carriage, I went into the house once more to look at the rooms for what might be the last time.

When I came out, my husband was already sitting in the carriage holding the reins. Some old people sat behind him. They started, Ida and I followed on foot, pushing the wheel-barrow, while Bibi ran around us, long ears and red tail flying, barking with delight, the only one of us to find the expedition great fun. A peasant led the way along a field to where the trees began, away from the noise and shouting and we penetrated deep into the woods until we reached the clearing.

In a short time we had pitched a sort of gypsy-camp, and tried to light a fire as rain began to fall. We lay back silently in our chairs on the grass, uneasily on watch. Having arranged some rudimentary comforts, and reassured the children, whose nervousness was growing, we started to cook. Hours passed and night had fallen when a car suddenly stopped nearby and we heard footsteps approaching. For a moment we thought that we were to be allowed to return home. But this hope was disappointed by the appearance of a group of sinister men in civilian clothes. We could not make out whether they were Russian deserters or Ukrainians. They herded us together pistol in hand, uttering rough threats, and questioned us in aggressive tones about our identity and our reason for hiding in the woods.

The engineer said he was a locksmith, to make himself appear as menial as possible, and the farmer that he was a labourer. When they came to my husband my heart stood still as I heard him say: "I am the owner of Kerzendorf and also of these woods." When he was interrupted by the engineer, who in order to protect him explained to the interrogator in an eloquent pantomime that Freddy was very sick from heart trouble, my husband protested irritably: "Let me speak, please. Why should I conceal the truth? I have nothing to hide."

At this point the interrogator was pushed aside by his companions who brutally demanded watches and jewelry that none of us had brought along. Every bag, every bundle was opened, sacks turned upside down, pockets inside out, and their contents greedily torn from us. I was confronted by a small dark man with gleaming teeth, who wore a dressing-gown round his neck like a muffler. A nightdress was thrown over his arm and handkerchiefs were stuffed into his pockets. When he fished a comb out from one of my pockets and I explained that I needed it, he handed it back to me with a low bow.

Suddenly he gave a cry of exultation at the discovery of a worthless ring with a piece of coral in it, that a friend had found in a Lisbon street and given me for good luck. When he bit on the coral and realized that it was not a gem, he threw it away in disgust, swearing and brandishing his pistol at us.

Our men were unarmed and helpless. The women and children cried and sobbed. The bandits threw things to each other, volubly discussing their value, and at last packed their loot into their car, harnessed our precious horses to a carriage, and drove off. In the darkness Freddy silently climbed into our cart and went to sleep, joined by a Bibi intimidated for the first time in her life by the foreigners' strange behaviour. Others lay around on rugs, or like Ida and myself sought shelter under the trees, opening an umbrella against the downpour of rain. We slept little from our fear of new assaults and from the disturbing sound of shooting that was steadily growing louder.

Slowly, black night turned into grey dawn as we woke to a scene of wild disorder; clothes, food, broken luggage, single shoes littered the ground, while half buried under miscellaneous

95

objects a little picture was lying face downward in the middle of the expanse of wet grass. On picking it up I found it to be a drawing by Gian Battista Tiepolo, a present from my father which I was so accustomed to taking with me wherever I went, that I had even brought it on this dangerous expedition. It had been at the bottom of my suit-case and the bandits had tossed it away.

A boy whom we had sent back for news arrived to report that there was no question of our returning home for many days and advised us to leave the woods immediately, as yesterday's robbers were on their way back for the rest of our possessions. Now that we had lost the horses we might be safer walking on the main highway to Ludwigsfelde, the little town nearby, where Freddy's doctor lived in a small house with his wife and child, who could perhaps put us up for a few days.

We assembled what was left of our scattered possessions. They were now difficult to transport, as the thieves had taken most of our suit-cases and other containers, and the carts had become useless without horses. We hid the chairs, a bottle of whiskey and a sack of potatoes in the undergrowth. The rest went into the wheelbarrow, which I tried to relieve of the bigger pans, pleading with Ida and winning, though at the cost of making her very bad-tempered. We decided to divide ourselves into small groups so as to attract less attention, and we three started off on our own, soon losing the others.

As we came out of the woods, but long before we reached the road, we heard a sound of traffic and loud singing. When we came up to the highway we could hardly believe our eyes. A gigantic carnival was streaming along. There was a succession of trucks filled with drunken and laughing soldiers, holding open parasols and wearing womens' hats and scarves, officers driving in cars, liberated prisoners, Poles and villagers driving cattle, who pushed through the cars with intent faces, in a hurry to get on as fast as possible. I recognized a little black dog-cart with red wheels. I remembered my father driving it, as it flew past

96

us filled with unknown men who must have stolen it from our stables, followed by another carriage decorated all over with Italian flags and packed with Italians singing Neapolitan songs. Some French prisoners called out to me:

"Going to join the Americans?"

"Can we get through to Ludwigsfelde?" we called back.

"Yes, no fighting in this area just now." So on we went.

The road of which we knew every stone and tree by heart, as it had been our daily route to the railway station, had become oddly unfamiliar. It was no longer the road to Berlin or back to Kerzendorf. It was taking us away from home towards liberty, or was it to new danger? We had no choice but to trudge wearily on.

As it started to rain heavily, Bibi, who had been trotting along contentedly beside me, became so wet, her long hair clinging to her body, that she sat down in misery and indignation and refused to take another step. I had to pick her up and carry her under one arm, shifting my suit-case to the other, while behind me, separated from me by struggling masses of people, walked Freddy and Ida pushing the wheelbarrow.

I was exhausted and nearing the end of my strength when I was accosted by an old man pulling a little cart containing a few potatoes.

"Let me put your bag on my cart," he said, "for we seem to be going in the same direction."

It was a relief to hear a friendly voice and to be rid of the suit-case. I had no more strength to carry it. We walked on the side of the road, away from the cars, trying not to be forced apart by men and women brushing past us in an hypnotic trance, precipitated by a sense of liberation they were as yet unable to believe. "Where are you going?" I called out to a woman from a neighbouring village who was pushing a baby-carriage containing two small children. She looked at me with a face filled with horror.

"West, to my mother, away from the Russians."

Two Yugo-Slavs who used to visit the people living with us, waved from afar, taking long strides. "Going home," they shouted.

Belgians, Dutch, Poles, Ukrainians, German-speaking people from the Black Sea or Rumania, where they had lived peacefully until they had been uprooted and transported to their 'home country', where they had found no place to live or work, German soldiers in ill-fitting civilian clothes obviously borrowed to rid themselves of the uniforms in which they would be bound to be taken prisoner, and all the others whose origin I could not define, were struggling along to return to the homes from which war had separated them by force.

The local population had feared above all things that this motley crowd would resort to acts of vengeance, but as all were equally sick of violence, they were as little tempted as animals in full flight to steal anything that would have impeded them in their determination to get back to their pre-war lives as soon as possible. Only bicycles and horses were in demand. Money was useless, the currency for payment and bartering was the ex-prisoners' stock of chocolate and cigarettes which had been distributed to them by the Red Cross.

A group of wounded and limping German prisoners in torn uniforms, led by Russian guards, looked like an illustration of Napoleon's army after the battle of the Beresina.

"Look," said my old companion, pointing with his chin, for now he was pulling his cart with both hands while I was hiding the trembling Bibi under my coat. "If my king had governed Germany we should have had no war and suffered no defeat."

"Who is your king?" I inquired politely, although I was at that moment trying to avoid being run over by a procession of carriages full of women singing an incomprehensible national anthem at the top of their voices. "I am a monarchist," he explained, "faithful to the Royal House of Saxony. I have only come to live in this foreign country of Prussia a year ago, when Dresden was pulverized by bombs. As my father and grandfather before me, I was a footman in the palace of Dresden until 1918, when the Royal family was driven away against the wish of the population. What a court, what splendour! How wise and kind a man was the last king!"

He was devoted to the Margrave of Saxony, a son of the late king, and while a long column passed us singing the Marseillaise so loudly it almost drowned our words, we talked of the exquisite taste with which the Prince had arranged the interior of Moritzburg, the austere little palace with its four towers reflected in a calm lake. The palace contained unique collections, among which the eighteenth-century Meissen made at the factory founded by his forefathers was outstanding.

While mechanically avoiding the vehicles around us, we exchanged reminiscences about the fragile Saze figurines and dishes he knew so well from having served at court dinners. He remembered the color of the tureens and plates, the arrangement of the flowers and the Royal Palace's collection of table linen that comprised the oldest and most complete sets in the world since they had first been woven in the sixteenth century and had accumulated in huge quantities in the Palace's vaults ever since.

We were sharing each other's favourite subject, and had become allies against the sea of anonymous humanity through which we were trying to cut a path.

"Where are you going?" I asked him.

He was returning to Ludwigsfelde where he was now living with his daughter and son-in-law, a skilled workman.

"I went out to find something to eat, but could only dig up some potatoes. What about you?"

When I told him about our plan of going to the doctor's house, he warned me against it.

"Their little villa offers no protection against passers-by. Soldiers can go in and out as they please. I know of a safer place, a flat on the second floor of the house we live in. It is standing empty, and the owners have given me the key."

The city of Ludwigsfelde was overcrowded with masses of soldiers impatiently shouting because their orders in Russian were not being understood. Most of them were short and fat, with thick noses and lips, their hair closely cropped, walking uncouthly with legs far apart and unable to communicate with their compatriots the thin-boned lean Mongols who were darting about rapidly and spoke no word of Russian.

It was a relief to get away from the jolting and pushing crowd when our guide, Justus Eber, led us up the grey cement stairs into a little flat in one of the tenement blocks built for workers' families. The building was part of one of the many housing estates constructed for factory employees all over the country under the Weimar Republic.

The rooms, that seemed a haven to us, were arranged like a suite in a hotel, consisting of a bedroom with two beds, a sitting-room furnished in light colored wood, a bathroom in which of course no water was running, and a little modern kitchen with every sort of gadget, although in the absence of gas and electricity, the stove and the ice-box had a merely decorative value.

Despite our exhaustion, and to the ceaseless sound of gun-fire, Justus Eber insisted on introducing us to his wife, daughter and son-in-law. The latter had just been stopped by the Russians on his way home and when he declared himself to be a worker, their response had been: "You proletarians must tell us where the fat lazy directors of the factory are hiding, so that we can kill them for you."

He was enraged by being called a proletarian—and why should he be jealous of a director? Even if their income was higher than his, they worked hard enough for it, and he himself would have become one in time. "This old-fashioned propaganda does not impress us," he said deprecatingly.

On the same floor as ourselves a fair tall refugee from East Prussia, whose husband had been lost somewhere in Russia, and who was forcibly separated from the rest of her family, was living with a young twenty-year-old Frenchman, one of the many foreign workmen brought to the Ludwigsfelde factory under the Nazi system of forced labour. They seemed to be very much in love and were quite unaffected by events about them, except for a deadly fear that their happiness would end if he were ordered home. Their romance had been dangerous for them until that moment, for had it been discovered he would have been sent to a punishment camp and she to prison. In the present upheaval they were no longer obliged to conceal their feelings and could stay together undisturbed. As I went by their open door he was helping her to hang laundry on a clothes-line. He was singing and she was laughing.

Introductions continued, and even in the confusion of the first evening, we could sense the relative status accorded to the different occupants of the house, and the way they conformed to the same social patterns that exist all over the world, in villages and small towns, bathing resorts and Royal Courts.

Eber was a worldly-wise and cynical old man with a brilliant past, the equivalent of a retired Minister of State, to whom material matters were of supreme importance. His son-in-law was an ambitious man who believed in his career and was indifferent to his colorless, conventional wife.

An old woman, a former nurse of the Daimler factory who had great medical knowledge, lived surrounded by photographs of former directors of the factory who had been her patients and were as glamorous to her as Royalty to others. Her position was influential, because it was assumed that as the local butcher's sister she would soon be able to dispense meat to her favorites.

A young man upstairs with beautiful violet eyes was disliked because he wistfully kept apart from the others to play Tchaikovsky to himself. He hated the factory, the town, everybody, including himself, and was kept alive by the ambition to become a hairdresser in Berlin, so that he could make enough money to go to night clubs and concerts.

Then there was a married couple with three children who

101

quarrelled, and another couple named Luck, who were devoted to each other and unhappy at not having a child.

We were faint with hunger when we were at last left alone in possession of our rooms, for as our tins had been stolen in the woods, we had nothing to eat in over forty-eight hours and the Ebers could only supply us with two or three potatoes.

"Is this all I get after these exertions?" Ida complained in a very bad temper. From force of habit she held us responsible for her food and would not recognize the changed circumstances. But we gave her credit for her foresight. We should have been lost without the pans she had insisted on bringing and which we now used to warm our scanty supper.

Eber's daughter came up to suggest that Ida and I should spend the night in the air-raid shelter downstairs, where the women of the house had gathered for greater safety, guarded by their men who were standing on watch near the entrance. We preferred to remain upstairs with my husband whose heart was troubling him, and lay on our beds in our coats in a state of tension, with neither electric light nor candles to relieve the oppressive darkness, and nothing to distract us from the sound of shooting and drunken voices and the flash of machine-guns against the darkness.

In the middle of the night shouting broke out across the street, to end in a furious pounding at our door. Ida and I got up and crept down the stairs to take refuge in the cellar—but to get there we were obliged to pass the lightly built wooden door that alone separated us from the intruders, who were yelling orders on its other side and threatening to shoot us if it was not immediately opened. To our terror, the stairs creaked abominably, and one of our men appeared at the foot of the staircase to warn us to be quick. Ida whispered bitterly we should have done better to have stayed upstairs, while for one dreadful second the menacing voices were only a few inches away.

When we had got safely past, a man carrying a flashlight guided us through a huge empty coal cellar, and then through passages into a large dormitory where women and children were lying and sitting on mattresses. They showed us a small door leading to a backyard by which we could escape if the front door was forced. Suddenly the whole house resounded from top to bottom from a tremendous crash. The soldiers had violently kicked in the entrance, but on entering they had found themselves confronted with the men of the house standing in a line, ready to kill or be killed, determined to defend their women. The Russians, who had expected an easy victory, were so taken aback at the sight of this phalanx, that cursing noisily they left for the next house. On my way upstairs to tell my husband that we were safe, the lovely East Prussian peered out of a door I was passing, and behind her in the dark I saw the outline of her young lover. "Has anything happened?" she inquired. "I thought I heard a noise?" Screams, the splintering of wood, the stamping of boots on the stairs, nothing had been able to distract them from each other, and when I reassured her, they both vanished back into their dreamland.

We spent the rest of the night in the cellar, with the men at the broken door constantly warding off new groups of soldiers in search of adventure or loot. When at last an uneasy dawn broke, the men brought planks to repair the entrance, and a thin partition again gave us the illusion of protection from the outside world.

In the morning we had no bread nor potatoes left and all food in the town had been requisitioned. So we decided to venture out to discuss the situation with Freddy's doctor. Before leaving the house, I persuaded my husband to take off his tie and put a scarf around his neck, for to Russians the wearing of a collar, or, even worse, a necktie, was a deliberate flaunting of class distinction and, as such, a hostile act. He disliked doing what I asked, and, even so, his coat and shoes, though old and worn, were of a different make to those of working people, so that I trembled at the remarks shouted after him and did not breathe freely until we had arrived safely at the doctor's.

103

We found him in a state of collapse. Alone in a little house from which there was no escape from intruders, he had been unable to fight off the Russian soldiers or to defend his wife from them. She was now sobbing in her room, in which the furniture and mirrors had been overturned and broken.

"Where can we find bread?" we asked.

"A baker has opened, but there is already a long queue waiting in front of the shop," we were told.

I started out, keeping close to the walls of the houses, for the streets were crowded with soldiers who for the first time in their lives had learned of the existence of bicycles. To ride them was as blissful for these men as a new mechanical toy is to a child. They shouted with delight when all went well, and yelled in distress when they fell off or rode at full speed into a wall. No bicycle was safe from their clutches, and as there were not enough to go round, they fought over them amongst themselves.

At the next corner I found a long queue of weary women waiting for their turn at the bakery, so I stood at a considerable distance from the shop and for more than two hours hopefully watched the distribution of loaves. Suddenly there was a commotion and slamming of doors, and a man came to announce gruffly: "No more supplies, but some may be coming in later." A deep sigh of disappointment passed through us all at the same moment.

In the hours of waiting that now began we exchanged stories with our neighbours about our experiences during the last few days. They were all, but for details, terribly and monotonously the same.

"Look at that girl," said a young woman, "none of us will speak to her after her behaviour yesterday."

It seemed that she had left her door open purposely to attract soldiers to where she was lying in bed in an alluring nightdress, in the hope of finding a protector who would give her food. Two Russians who had entered for a moment stood speechless. Then both spat in disgust, using a coarse word, shocked to the core by a woman who could offer herself to them. They went on to the room next door, from where soon came cries for help from the girl's grandmother, aged sixty-nine. Her valiant defence of her honour had made her more attractive than the pretty, too willing girl.

There was a sound of crunching gravel and grinding gears, and a large truck packed with soldiers stopped in front of the baker's shop. Twenty or thirty of them got out headed by an officer in charge, a man with a coarse expression and glittering teeth of solid gold. He announced that women were needed to peel potatoes in a soldiers' camp and asked for volunteers. Their work would be paid for with soup and potatoes.

The girl next to me whispered: "My sister was taken away four days ago on the same pretext and has not returned yet. A friend of mine escaped and brought back stories of what happened to her and the others."

When a frail, hungry-looking, white-haired woman lifted her arm to offer her services, the golden-toothed one did not even glance at her, but pointed his pistol at the young girl, the would-be seducer of conquerors, of whom the others had been talking. As she did not move, he gave a rough command. Two soldiers came to stand beside him, four more walked right and left of the single file of women until they reached her and ordered her to get into the truck. She was in tears as she was brutally shoved forward, followed by others who were protesting helplessly.

The men were approaching the spot where I stood. For one icy moment the leading man caught my eye, and petrified with fear, I looked down at my feet, in a desperate attempt to escape attention.

"Quick, follow me," the girl behind me whispered in my ear. "Turn round, walk after me and do not look back."

I obeyed automatically, and followed her down the column of frightened women to the end of the street, round the corner, across a short alley leading to the doctor's backyard and into his house. We could hardly believe that we were safe and held each other's hands incredulously.

The doctor's wife kept us for a time and soothed us with unforgettable kindness. A number of girls and women were waiting nervously for the doctor to beg him either to remove an unwanted child or for a remedy against syphilis they had caught in Asiatic embraces.

"It is a virulent form of sickness, unknown in this part of the world," she said; "it would be difficult to cure even if we were lucky enough to have any penicillin."

"Why then," asked my friend, "are the Russians supposed to have health far superior to that of Western Europeans?"

"Because their constitutions are so strong that they recover from their illness which we would die from in terrible agony, and live to an old age even if they are not entirely healed."

Hours had passed since I left home, and it was an ordeal to go back, open the door and face Freddy, Ida and Bibi, who had been waiting hopefully for food, and, shaken and upset as I was, to be obliged to admit that I returned empty-handed. We had absolutely nothing left to eat and were in the first stages of starvation, the state of super-sensitivity which ascetics seek to induce through fasting.

They were sitting in a semi-obscurity of the late afternoon, for want of light.

When I told them about my escape from the crowd of soldiers, we were reminded of a dinner at the British Embassy in Berlin which I had once attended with my father. A guest seated opposite me at the beginning of the meal vanished during dinner without anyone noticing his departure. When he explained to his neighbour on his right that he was feeling sick, she quickly removed his plate and wine glasses, and motioned to a footman to take away his chair, and he had walked out unobserved and without leaving a trace behind him.

We were interrupted by Eber who came in great agitation to complain that he and his family were also without food. It was

106

too dangerous to rejoin the queue, so the only alternative, if we were not to die of starvation, was to fetch the sack of potatoes we had hidden in the undergrowth near our camp and then, with luck, to reach a field beyond the forest nearer Kerzendorf, where there were rows and rows of carrots covered by earth mounds for protection against frost, as a reserve of food for men and cattle in the early spring, before the earth yielded its fresh crops. The withered stalks of the plants are burned in large fires, when the potatoes have been dug up, and some of them are roasted in the embers and eaten deliciously hot in the cool October air.

As children, instead of using matches, we would kindle the fires with transparent flintstones which we found in the soil, bearing the delicate impression of shells or fern-leaves, the perfectly preserved fossils of life and vegetation hundreds of thousands of years old, dating back to the time when the austere little province of Brandenburg had alternately been the bottom of an ocean and the heart of a luxuriant tropical jungle. Enclosed in the dark room, as I now listened to the wild sounds outside, I felt as if our familiar surroundings were being swept away as radically as though another glacial period had begun or our world had collided with a wayward comet.

Chapter IX

ONCE AGAIN we were obliged to endure the recurrent nightmare of nocturnal confusion which varied only in detail. When we set out in the early morning, we forced ourselves to forget the terror of the night and concentrate on our errand.

As Mr. Eber, pulling a little rattling cart, Ida and I stepped out of the house, we were enveloped closely by a cold, heavy fog, that forced us to proceed carefully so as not to run into invisible beings or cars. After an hour and a half's walk we left the road at a point near Kerzendorf to take a cross-country path of which I knew every turning and stone. A shot was fired so near us that we stood aghast. "We are in the forbidden area occupied by the General and his tanks. The guards will kill us if we go on," said Mr. Eber in a shaking voice. As we could already make out the promised outlines of little mounds, we decided, after whispered deliberations, to leave the cart and crawl cautiously forward. We eluded two more shots, and a third that just grazed Mr. Eber, by lying flat on the ground before we crept forward inch by inch, with long intervals of waiting, interrupted by the sharp whining of bullets over our heads. It was unthinkable to any of us that we should give up what had started as a dreary search for food and had become a thoroughly exciting game. We were seized by the primitive hunting instincts of our neolithic ancestors. When at last we had reached our goal, we dared not stand up, but knelt, sending the soil flying in our eagerness to unbury the vegetables that we had come for, and to fill the three sacks which Mr. Eber had wisely brought along, before daylight made us visible to the soldiers. We could not resist eating for the first time in forty-eight hours, and after hastily cleaning the long pink carrots with a handker-chief, swallowed one after another feeling that never in our lives had we enjoyed a better meal. A bullet smacked into the other side of the mound which we were looting, and we began to crawl back as fast as we could, shoving the heavy sacks in front of us, until we reached the cart.

We loaded it with our prize and left Ida to guard it while I showed Mr. Eber the way to the clearing in the woods. We found the disorder of a few days before unchanged and the things which we had hidden undisturbed. Mr. Eber shouldered the bag of potatoes, I put the bottle of whiskey under my coat, and we picked up the two chairs lying on the grass intending to lay them on top of the sacks and pretend that we were simply carting dull bits of furniture. When we rejoined Ida, she grumbled at having been kept waiting.

We then went through a short period of acute danger, for we were obliged to walk upright in order to push the heavy cart forward on the rough path. When we had succeeded in reaching the highway unharmed by the flying bullets, I fell down ex-hausted near the ditch beside the road and leaned against a tree.

A voice spoke close from underneath my feet: "Who is there?"

Mr. Eber nearly let the bottle drop with which he was reviving his spirits, and bending down I saw a man lying at the bottom of the ditch, who lifted his head, then let it sink back. "Water," he pronounced with difficulty. We had only whiskey. I poured it between his lips while Ida held him up, and a little later, when he had opened his eyes, we got out some carrots for him. He sat up with an effort and seeing us covered with earth, and with dried leaves in our hair, he smiled and said wonderingly: "You look odd, where do you come from?"

Mr. Eber resented criticism and remarked coldly, "Of course we must look dignified when we return to Ludwigsfelde. Please allow me to clean your coat." He addressed me with a deferential politeness that was surprising in these circumstances. "I should be ashamed of myself if I had not thought of bringing a good clothes-brush along." He brushed me until I was spotless, and then turned his brush on Ida and himself with the same energy, and continued impatiently, "Now let's go home quickly for we will have nothing left if we share the little we have with the first person we come across"; and he glared in irritation down at the man lying there. The stranger complained of a badly injured leg, so that for the first time I had an opportunity to use the little first-aid kit that I had always carried with me since the beginning of the war. When we helped him out of the ditch, he was so weak that he could hardly walk; we saw he was thin and slight and that his narrow face with its high cheek-bones was very pale. "Could you help me along until I can get a lift," he begged, despite Mr. Eber's suspicious glances. "I want to reach a French prisoners' camp and from there I hope to get further transportation."

As we pushed the cart into the road, two Russians appeared with rifles over their shoulders and shouting incomprehensibly at us, threw the chairs off the cart and tore at the precious sacks. To our astonishment, the young man talked back at them in fluent Russian with so much conviction that they shrugged their shoulders and made an impatient gesture ordering us to move on.

His name was Fedja. He was the son of a Russian mother and a Polish father, and had been a prisoner since 1941 in France for having done resistance work. He had just escaped from the concentration camp where he had been interned during the most impressionable period of his youth, from his nineteenth to his twenty-third year. He told me of the horrors he had suffered and witnessed, of the day on which his best friend had been dragged from his side to be gassed. Three days before he had killed a hated guard with his own hands before leaving the camp. He spoke without emotion, without any appeal for sympathy, and showed no signs of obsession or bitterness. I

110

was startled by his attitude and shocked at his lack of indignation, for I believed that although one was morally obliged to accept the inevitable with calm, one should recognize cruelty from whatever side it came and never give way to it without opposition, or without inner revolt if an outward reaction were made impossible. I told him angrily that apathy and resignation in face of oppression was a form of sin. It amounted to complicity in a denial of basic human values.

He answered: "Violence is the essence of our time. It is as much part of our modern existence to be in constant danger of destruction as security was the norm during the latter half of the nineteenth century. Think of the millions of men and women in camps and prisons in Germany, in the Balkans, in Spain, in Russia, who have had to reckon with it."

He stood still and tugged at my arm until I turned to him and said angrily: "Anyone who has not lost his home and who is not separated from those he loves is an exception. Are you one of them?"

I pointed to the church spire of Kerzendorf in the distance, and told him that the sight of it made my heart beat faster, and that I hoped to return there soon. I added, nervously feeling that I must appear complacent to him, "I am now going back to my husband."

"I suppose some of you will remain on the shore and not be swept into this," he retorted petulantly. He made a gesture towards the scene around us, now distinct in the morning sunlight which was struggling through a white mist. A wounded man was being carried past on a litter, three soldiers and two women were drinking and drunk at a crossroad, many others were anxiously pressing forward. The scene resembled Callot's engravings or Goya's *Disasters of War*, with their burnt houses, peasants strung up from trees, corpses and carcasses lying on the ground while officers in elegant uniforms lead regiments by to the music of military bands. We were seeing re-enacted the tragedies and contrasts familiar to seventeenth-

111

century Europe, and realized how the sad tale of humanity repeats itself throughout the centuries.

"This stream," my companion was saying, "flows round the world swollen by innumerable victims of war and politics, by whole populations that have been driven out, in fact, by a great part of the inhabitants of the globe. They will be joined by those who after long years of war spent far from their own country have become unfit to find a place in a world shaken by social and spiritual upheavals. Men and women who are still secure never sleep without trembling at the flood they hear rushing by their windows."

"But," I tried to answer him, "if one is thrown into the waters, one can surely fight one's way out and succeed in taking root again?"

"I will not succeed," he answered, "for between Russia, Poland and France, I belong nowhere, nor will many others. Love and friendship are forces which we recognize to be the only stable elements in our existence, but even those cannot bind us to a place. In being critical towards our surroundings we have learned the rapture of moving on, of beginning again, of giving in to the supreme temptation of restlessness. Nostalgia of the East for those who once lived there is not comparable with the fascination of being a nomad ready for any adventure, impatient to escape again and again from meaningless habits and taboos."

My companion spoke fitfully, for his foot hurt him and he was limping badly. "I am planning to write a book in the same vein as the great novel *Simplizissimus*, that great autobiography of a young man in love with life written during the Thirty Years' War. He relates the story of his wanderings that led him from misery and starvation to towns glamorous and brilliant with court life and resounding to the rhythm of dancing and music. He tells of the varied chances of luck and ill-luck, of poverty and prosperity, that befell him. Like him I will write about my own feelings, but they are essentially the same for all men at all times, though my behaviour and habits are formed by the disintegration into which I was born. In the static world of yesterday an individual had to come to terms with a highly organized society, but today I myself am obliged to become solid if I am to be consistent in my beliefs and aims, so as not to dissolve in my fluid surroundings. The writers that preceded me gave a picture of their reactions to the intricacies of city life, sheltered from physical danger, in the certainty of inherited creeds; I, who am a part of the today that I love, know about new laws and hierarchies and burn to describe the richness and responsibility of personal experience, and become their successor as the historian of the road."

He waved to an approaching horse-drawn cart. It stopped, and while the passengers helped him in, he turned his pale face towards me: "I will put you in my book," he said and laughed. He leaned out and in a voice barely audible over the rumble of the wheels called "Au revoir" and was gone.

A peasant woman had been trying to attract my attention for some time. "Have you anything to barter for apples?" she asked, and we exchanged fruit for carrots to everyone's satisfaction and pride in having obtained a new item of food to bring home; it was a wonderful world in which such successes were possible.

A Dutchman asked us to show him the way, and accompanied us for a while. He was a pianist by profession, just escaped from a camp and married to an American, and was overcome with joy at being free to go back to his family and to his music. He made me uneasy by his advice to leave this part of the country at once. "Don't remain here," he warned. "Do not confuse the kindness and warmth of heart of individual Russians with their relentless system. Anyone who does not rigidly conform to it, as no one not brought up under its iron laws possibly can, is bound to be exterminated."

"But will they remain here for ever," I asked.

"Probably not," he thought, "but for you to stay is a dangerous gamble."

At the entrance of Ludwigsfelde I encountered a group of French prisoners who stopped me to say good-bye; one of them told me of his recent experiences in a punishment camp and said slowly: "I shall bring up my children in hatred of Germany for what Hitler did to France."

"What he has done to his own country is no better," retorted one of his companions, pointing to a row of burnt-out houses and to the people miserably straggling on around us.

When we got home, Freddy, and with him the whole household, welcomed us with relief, and was delighted by the load of carrots which solved our immediate problems. The successful expedition marked an important day for Freddy and me, for it was the first time that I had found myself more fitted to cope with difficulties than he was. In normal civilized life he had always been supreme, but I was less surprised by our present plight because I had always been suspicious of security from my childhood onwards. I felt that a part of the responsibility that until now had lain on his shoulders alone had shifted to mine, and felt happy to think that I could contribute something new and necessary to our joint existence at this moment of stress. My joy was so great that nothing could disturb it, not even the raw wind that made me shiver during the night as we stood in the back-yard hiding behind the fir trees.

We awoke to a feeling that something had completely changed, something pleasant, relaxing and delicious. But what was it? Then we realized that the gunfire had stopped. The day had begun unaccompanied by its thunder. Neighbours brought news that Berlin had capitulated, but the encircled troops were still fighting around the Zoo fortress which lay near the building containing our apartment. It must surely have been destroyed by now. It was agony not to know if Hedi, the friend living in it, or old Pauline who had taken refuge there, were still alive.

From the window we saw a long procession of tired and foot-sore German prisoners. All of them were part of the last reserve of middle-aged men drafted at the end of the war when even the physically unfit were called. Women came out of the houses to bring them bread and water, and I watched a Russian guard dismount from his own bicycle and hand it over to a prisoner who could hardly walk, helping him to mount it with fraternal compassion.

Meanwhile food had given us new energy and we were capable of enjoying the present once more. Until yesterday our only furniture had been beds of the cruel kind often found in central Europe fitted with mattresses divided in three sections each of which has painfully sharp corners. Now we had the luxury of two comfortable chairs in which we could spend long quiet hours reading the books that I had brought along in spite of protests. Freddy read Spanish history and I became immersed in Eckhardt, the twelfth-century mystic, great writer, founder of the sect of 'God's Friends'. I had been taught by my father to love his writings, in which he expressed his confidence in the Deity and his acceptance of life. My father always kept the mediæval priest's books by him, and when he was overtaken by sudden death he was holding *About the Heart's Wisdom* in his hands.

It was surprising to find how easy it was for men of that century to travel. An obscure monk from Constance had found it possible to visit Rome, Paris and Canterbury, and everywhere discoursed with his contemporaries in Latin, the universal language of educated people at that time. Church and courts had created widespread mutual understanding through the web of their connections, so that even after war reconciliation was possible. How much darker is our present age when every nation lives in ignorance of its neighbours in separate worlds, and provincialism is developed to such an extreme that recently in Germany and now in Russia a citizen is considered a potential traitor to the state merely for being acquainted with a foreigner.

The next day was the fourth of May. We were so exhausted

by nightly disturbances that we could only see, not feel, the loveliness of the day.

Neighbours came with rumours: Admiral Dönitz was negotiating, Hitler had died, Goebbels had taken poison. General Paulus, who had been taken prisoner with his troops at Stalingrad, General Seydlitz, who during the last six months had spoken on the wireless to the German Army from a Russian camp, exhorting it to put a stop to the war by revolution, were supposed to have arrived in Berlin. Was all this true? Though we were only twenty miles away from the capital the distance was impenetrable, as there was no means of communication.

Towards evening I found Ida crying bitterly. Through her sobs she said that the apartment we were now occupying was exactly what she would have liked had she married and founded a family instead of going to work in the capital. Today she revolted against her spinsterhood and bitterly regretted the life she might have led. During these early days of May we heard on all sides that, when the conquerors moved out of houses they had requisitioned, these were looted by the population. In the neighbouring village of Lowen the Ukrainian servants had saved themselves from execution as collaborators by showing the Russian soldiers where their absent masters had walled up the silver and wine. The village people had followed in their wake, taken what they wanted and thrown the rest out of the windows in an orgy of destruction. Greed proved stronger than attachment to a family that had owned the estate for three hundred years. It was imperative that we should go over to Kerzendorf and find out if there was any chance that we could return there soon. I set out escorted by Mr. Eber, in fear of the soldiers and of what I should find at home, and only slightly comforted by the pleasure of wearing a light gay dress I had taken with me to Ludwigsfelde. There was less traffic now. Only a few trucks and an occasional car drove past, splashing us with mud, and people were trundling along little dog-carts filled with their belongings. Groups of German prisoners lay listlessly along

116

the roadside. To reach the part of Kerzendorf that had been evacuated and was now open to civilians, we took a track that had been our favourite riding route because of its soft sand that was ideal for galloping. It was sweet with the scent of acacias and led through green meadows where bees hummed and the songs of birds filled the air. From the distance came the lowing of cows abandoned and unmilked.

The peasants we came across were admirable for the energy and foresight with which they had started to sow and replant, but they irritated us when they spoke about politics. "Conditions are worse than before," they said. "We were better off under Hitler"—never considering the cause that had brought their disasters upon them.

Sentries would not let us approach the house and the farmyard was still full of tanks. No one knew when the unit would leave. We sent a message to Monk to tell him of our arrival and to ask him to fetch us in Ludwigsfelde the moment the troops were ordered away. As we reached the centre of Kerzendorf we found consternation, for a few hours earlier Wilhelm, our gardener and gamekeeper, had committed suicide by hanging himself from a tree in the woods, having first slashed the wrist arteries of his wife and three-year-old son, refusing to leave them behind him in a world of strife and disorder. They had been found in time to revive them, but he himself was stark and cold. Despite his stalwart looks, Wilhelm was a sensitive man, whom his much younger but ailing wife had worn out by her nervousness. Yesterday drunken soldiers had upset his treasured beehives, used his jars of preserves as shooting targets and driven the couple and the child out of the house. He had not been able to stand the strain of these repeated scenes and now lay on the ground covered with a blanket.

I knew that the brutality of this event as well as the loss of a close collaborator would be a cruel shock to my husband. On my return to Ludwigsfelde I took pains to break the news to him as quietly and gently as possible.

117

Ida woke me that night at twelve-thirty. When I had slipped on my coat and run to the head of the staircase there came the sound of splintering glass, cracking wood and a heavy thud at the back of the house. Freddy was indignant when I compelled him to dress, since whatever happened he hated being disturbed. We heard a hubbub of voices that seemed friendly and someone called up reassuringly. Two young Frenchmen had come home from a visit long after curfew and had broken into the house to escape the pursuit of the Russian soldiers.

Freddy spoke seriously to me about this incident as we were walking in the back garden next morning in the grey fresh air. It was an untidy place, strewn with litter and with washing hanging up on clothes-lines, but we felt safer there at night and unobserved during the daytime. "You must not allow yourself to get so upset and disturb me in this thoughtless way," he admonished me. "In your impatience you forget that we must have rest and sleep and preserve our sanity through these weeks. What we are passing through is nothing but a period of transition."

I explained that my conception of the peace I longed for was to be once more free from fear and the feeling of being hunted; I wanted to see windows shining out freely into the dark west instead of being muffled by blackout; I dreamed of the time when pictures and works of art would come back to daylight from the cellars and caves, and to live to see a new confidence in the security of possessions.

I went away to read, with Bibi on my lap; she rested her pointed nose on my elbow while I became absorbed in James Joyce's description of the conflicts and problems of his youth in Dublin, in the *Portrait of the Artist as a Young Man*. It evoked a memory of Joyce as I had seen him one late afternoon at Beatrice Guinness' house in London. The light had not yet been turned on when he entered as noiselessly as a ghost. He spoke in a low voice about Italo Svovo, the Triestine writer he greatly admired, and about his own failing eyes which were invisible

118

behind the thick lenses of his glasses. He was leaving for Zurich the next day to consult an oculist.

One Sunday I made a short expedition to fetch some tulips and walked past the houses painted in a morose olive-green to camouflage them against air-attack, to the outskirts of Ludwigsfelde where little white cottages, now so perilous a shelter, lay among the flowering fruit trees. The tulip grower remarked as he cut the flowers, "Once the railroads start functioning again food will be distributed and things will get better."

As I walked back, holding the cool leaves and long stems ending in closed scarlet and yellow buds, I passed a garden where a girl was working. To escape attention she had dressed like a boy, or so she thought, but the trousers only accentuated her round body, her tiny high-heeled shoes were undeniably feminine and the masculine jockey cap did not hide her pink and white face. She stood digging between two rows of high tulips in a charming little orchard lit by almond trees in blossom. It was like a décor for the opening scene of a musical comedy and every second one expected her to break into a song to the strains of an orchestra.

At dinner time the butcher's sister brought us a present of potato pancakes, a popular dish in Northern Germany, and at this moment a special delicacy, since it had been fried in fat, now almost unobtainable, which her brother had saved from a meal he had cooked the day before for Russian officers.

A girl arrived whose cousin had a friend who had a friend who owned a wireless. She could not give us much news. Munich had capitulated, but fighting was still going on in Hamburg, and what about our own vicinity? What had been decided in San Francisco? What about the war in Japan? She did not know, but told us that she had just heard a man in the street offer a woman to a Russian in return for a payment in meat. "Is she your wife?" the soldier wanted to know, for if she were

119

he would have refused the bargain. But when the man answered "No," he was given five pounds of beef and then led the Russian to where the woman was.

We were obliged to risk another visit to Kerzendorf to buy fresh vegetables which were now in season. I crossed a square where a rostrum had been erected for a political demonstration. It was decorated in glaring red, festooned with flags of yet another red that clashed with the first. Next to it was a grave with a simple wooden tablet bearing the names of five Russian soldiers who had been killed there only a fortnight earlier. When I walked on I saw the same Russians who broke savagely into people's houses every night, laughing and playing with little boys and girls who had complete confidence in them. On the highway we passed flocks of people who, having fled from Berlin before the siege, were now streaming back in great numbers. Amongst them we came across Mr. Fest, the refugee living in our house. I begged him to inquire about our apartment and the friend inhabiting it, and he promised to bring back an answer.

In Kerzendorf I found Mrs. Wilhelm recovered from her wound and silently sitting in front of the house. Anna Fisher, who used to be my playmate when I was a child, called to me from a window and asked me into her house. She was the ill-treated wife of a drunkard who had run into debt and who a few days before had confessed to having been a secret member of the Communist Party for years. "Now everybody is equally poor," announced Mrs. Fisher, looking at me with a delighted expression.

A peasant's wife, who invited us into her kitchen to sell us part of the mountains of spinach she was cooking for her family, told us that the Germans had organized a voluntary police force called 'Selfprotection', with the object of fighting anarchy and trying to control the wholesale transference of food to larger towns in order to conserve potatoes and wheat for next year's planting. They warned us of the dishonesty of a great number of

120

these men who used their position to rob people of food they wanted for themselves.

We left in fear of losing the little food we had acquired and, nervously carrying our sacks of spinach, we walked warily through the woods. They were alive with men and women busily gathering sticks into tidy heaps to take home for firewood. At the entrance to Ludwigsfelde, a girl fell into the hands of two men ten steps ahead of us, who took away her bundle in spite of her cries of protest. As they approached the tree where I had hidden I dodged them successfully by running quickly down a side-road and took a roundabout way that brought me safely home.

There I found the Protestant minister and the Catholic priest, both intelligent and broadminded men and not in the least antagonistic to each other, who had come to visit my husband. They made every effort to help the population and were as fearless in the way they tried to influence Russian and local Communist authorities as they had formerly been under the Nazis. They were disappointed that we had no more news than they. The only person in town, they said, whose wireless worked was the headmaster of the Ludwigsfelde school.

After the priests had gone, I went to see him and was shown to a little house on which, to my surprise, a red flag was displayed. The schoolmaster was out and I found his wife bandaging her fifteen-year-old son, at whom a soldier had shot by mistake, while she complained miserably that she did not know how to feed her family of four children. Only music came from the wireless, though earlier there had been a translation of a speech by Mr. Churchill.

"I never listen," she answered sullenly to my questions. "They all talk too much." When her husband appeared he started explaining in ardent self-justification, how he had originally been a Socialist, and later had left the Protestant church to join the Nazi party. As I said nothing, he looked at

121

me: "Socialist, National-Socialist, Communist," he said, "what I really am is an individualist."

Next morning, which was the eighth of May, we were woken up by an unusual stir in the streets, motor horns were hooting and truck-loads of soldiers were singing in high spirits. This activity went on all day, even when a thunderstorm broke and darkened the sky with pelting rain. We avoided going out and tried in vain to interpret the mysterious signs from our windows, but they were like a book written in an unfamiliar language; we could not guess their meaning.

After the storm, the day was transparently clear until far into the evening. We were lying on our beds looking at the outline of a fir tree black against the liquid turquoise sky in which gleamed a solitary star. There was a knock and the young East Prussian woman looked in. "My French friend has just told us that an armistice was signed at six o'clock last night," she said in a casual tone and then closed the door. It was in this matter-of-fact manner, as trivial gossip, that we heard of the end of the war, the end of death and hatred. We had waited so long and had often pictured it as a spectacular event, marked by a snowstorm of leaflets and a festive chime of bells.

Half an hour later Mr. Eber, his son-in-law and the Lucks from above came to discuss the news until late in the night. The evening now no longer brought the blazing of electric light but a veil of darkness that made sewing and reading impossible and wireless and movies unknown. We could not sleep like the birds when the sun went down. When night fell, people drew together for an endless exchange of ideas and speculations. Friendships are often formed in the quiet hours after midnight, in a bar or at a party, when professional duties have been laid aside, and there are no appointments or telephones to distract from the enchanting discovery of another person or a new aspect of oneself. It was exactly this mood that was created by our present circumstances. It brought a heightened awareness and sympathy

122

that would later make many men and women look back to troubled times as the most important in their lives.

The rhythm of our days had changed as well as that of the nights, for office and professional work, sports and social activities had ceased. Women could no longer shop, cooking consisted in a simple boiling of potatoes. As there were no appointments, no buses or trains to catch, hurry had become needless and unaccustomed leisure was created for people who had been driven from one task to another without respite as far back as they could remember. In the long hours of waiting while bread was being distributed or in walking from one place to another there was ample time for reflection and observation. The search for food made all former worries irrelevant, especially as it was impossible to imagine an unforeseeable future. It was the present moment alone that counted. Even if all were weak from hunger, senses were no longer dulled by pettiness; for many it was the first time that they had ever become properly alive to the beauty of nature and to ideas outside of their usual range.

The visitors stayed late. In the streets outside there was continued music and speeches relayed from loudspeakers. I was told of an order that all men in Ludwigsfelde had to report on the next day to the Russian Kommandatura, where they were to be put to work in clearing away rubble, that would have been a deadly exertion for my husband. The news kept me awake all night. When I went to the doctor's house before seven o'clock in the morning to beg him for a certificate testifying that Freddy was too ill to work, I found the doctor and his wife still asleep and the house shut. I waited for a long time on a bench in the garden, anxiously wondering whether the doctor would have the courage to give me the necessary certificate. Slowly the exquisite promise of spring in the early morning air soothed me and gave me the strength to convince the doctor once he was awake, to write out the few words I required.

I had just given the certificate to Freddy when we heard a

123

whistle under the window, and looking out cautiously saw Monk, who had come to report that the tank unit had left the evening before. He told us that we must hurry home at once for a rumour was circulating that we had abandoned Kerzendorf, and the village people might be tempted by the excuse to start looting.

Our dearest wish had unexpectedly been fulfilled. At last we could go home. Yet our joy was tempered by apprehension, for I was afraid of the hostility, losses and unprotected nights we would have to face even more in Kerzendorf than in Ludwigsfelde, for in our own small community we were naturally well known and it would be more difficult to hide. Freddy felt nothing but relief at being able to go back. "You will see now that the fighting is over, life is soon certain to return to normal," he said while dressing and packing. Mrs. Luck asked me to come to their room to impress on me how dangerous they considered it for us to return to Kerzendorf and to offer me a refuge with them in case of need. The whole household gathered to say good-bye, and escorted us down the stairs into the street, where we saw the East Prussian and her French friend waving from an upper window and calling out, "We will visit you soon." Then Mr. Eber, Monk, Ida and I started off, pushing the wheelbarrow with Freddy's hats balanced on top of it and Bibi galloping around us.

Chapter X

In Kerzendorf soldiers loafed about the closed entrances to the garden, each proudly wearing four, five or six wrist-watches on their arms, like women displaying diamond bracelets. They called out to us to ask if we had any watches, but let us go on to the house.

A scene of pandemonium confronted us, although the general had kept his word and done everything in his power to protect the house from looting. He had sealed off the bedrooms and library, testing the locks of the doors himself, and put an orderly in charge. Before he left at the head of his unit on the previous evening, he had taken the key of the house to the village mayor and with it a large diploma of a scientific society to which my father had belonged, bearing the signature of its founder Emperor William II, and had given orders that it should be returned to us in person.

The mayor was a white-haired old man who bore us no ill-will, although he had declared himself a Communist a fortnight before. He said he wished to co-operate with my husband in keeping order, but he had been powerless to carry out the general's instructions. During the night stray soldiers and villagers had climbed into the cellar through the smashed window-frames, and had broken open and looted cases of silver and trunks of clothes, both our own and the belongings of friends who had entrusted them to us for safe-keeping during the bombing.

It was as if a gale had swept through the rooms. Pictures had been slashed from top to bottom, cut-out faces of portraits still hung to the canvases by a thread, the floor was littered with my grandmother's wedding-gown, an old court-train in light blue and silver brocade, fancy dresses and pink hunting coats that we had left forgotten in the attic for years past. I enjoyed their discovery and their faded charm on that day; their possession was a great if short-lived pleasure, for soon they vanished for ever, stolen or taken by God knows whom.

Our secret hiding-place had not been discovered, much was still safe, but it seemed impossible ever to restore the house to what it had once been. Even the stove would not work. When we tried to cook a meal the pipe was found to be blocked and soon the smoke grew so thick we could hardly open our eyes. Masses of soldiers still swarmed ceaselessly in and out of the house like pigeons in a pigeonloft, looked about in surprised curiosity, picked up what they fancied and either carried it away or threw it out of the window.

One morning in June when I had been woken early by a cuckoo's song to a hot summer's day, the library door opened to let in two Russians. In my fright I hurried out to hide in a group of people standing in the farmyard, closely followed by the soldiers, who caught up with me and reproached me bitterly: "We only meant to ask you for water," they said. "You must be heartless to treat us so unkindly. Life is intolerable if we are continually avoided and people fly from us as if we were dangerous enemies." I was sorry to have hurt their feelings and asked them to have coffee with me. They were pleased and followed me into the Vesuvian fumes of the kitchen. One of the men told me of his homesickness for his mother from whom he had received no news for three years. Longing for her kept him from sleeping. The other made the gesture of stringing up someone on a scaffold: "Hitler!" he said and continued in his broken German. "Stalin should also hang, then we would all be happier."

When they had gone an unending stream of soldiers came to picnic in the garden, to peer in at the windows and enter by the doors. At times the confusion passed the limits of endurance,

126

my reason became a thin thread ready to snap at any moment, and the only escape was to withdraw into the more familiar world of books and contemplation. The scent of lilac was the same that I had known since childhood, nightingales sang with a sweetness so well remembered, that the strange presence of our Asiatic visitors seemed more unreal than abnormal.

The clergyman arrived to ask me to attend the funeral of an old village woman. It was to take place in the yard of her house in the presence of the entire village. As until now only our closest neighbours in the farmyard were aware of our return, our presence at the ceremony would be an opportune moment to make it public.

On my way, accompanied by Ida, I stopped to visit Mrs. Wilhelm, who had moved back into her house. I found her dressed in a black linen suit, which I recognized to my surprise as one that had been hidden in a suit-case in the cellar. "This is mine," I burst out. Mrs. Wilhelm looked at me indignantly: "Should I have allowed the strangers to take it?"

Still more puzzled I questioned her: "How did you happen to be present when the clothes were being stolen?"

At that she drew herself up like a queen and martyr and addressed me in the third person, in a respectful form of speech that oddly contrasted with her recent actions: "If Mrs. Horstmann wishes me to, I will strip them off my back immediately." I was thus constrained to beg her to keep the suit.

Soon afterward a refugee relative of hers entered with an umbrella on his arm as if he were just returning from the races. I gasped, for it was a present I had once given Freddy and a loss I had not yet discovered. However, I said nothing and we went on to the funeral, where I expressed my sympathy to the chief mourners and took the place of honour next to the mayor.

I said my prayers, and then, looking up as the clergyman began his sermon, my eyes fell on the grandson of the deceased, and round his neck saw a yellow woollen scarf with a brown checked pattern. My husband had bought one for each of us and it had amused us both to wear them on the same occasion. The boy's sister next to him had its twin around her waist, a cape belonging to my sister-in-law covered the shoulders of Mr. X, another wore Hedi's hat, a young man sported Freddy's suit—in fact, everyone present was wearing clothing that had once been ours. Ida pressed my arm, her eyes flashing. "We must call the police at once," she said indignantly, pointing to the girl opposite who was wearing one of her most cherished hats. Not for a moment did she doubt the power of justice. I turned to the mayor, who only mournfully shrugged his shoulders. When the service had ended, Ida went up to the culprit in a general silence to hiss at her, "Thief." The girl ran away instantly, the whole congregation dispersed, all carefully avoiding me. Only the clergyman remained, and warned me that it might be dangerous to complain.

On passing Mrs. Wilhelm's house on my way home, I caught a glimpse of her uncouth iron umbrella stand through her open front door and ran up the few steps: no one was in sight, my beautiful umbrella stood unguarded and I quickly seized it. When a few yards away I met the refugee coming towards me and called out a happy "Good morning." He was visibly startled to see me swinging the umbrella to and fro in my hand but said nothing. A friend is now—I hope he still is—in possession of the treasure that I had retrieved with such a glow of satisfaction.

The next day, May 14, when I was giving an English lesson to two girls, we were interrupted by the arrival of a soldier with orders that the inhabitants of Kerzendorf would fetch their bread ration from Ludwigsfelde, where it would be distributed. We walked over in a group, to stand patiently in a line gossiping and listening to rumours as women had done long ago in Biblical times, when they had fetched water at the fountain with pitchers on their shoulders. Mussolini had been executed in Milan, Stalin and Churchill had met in Berlin, the Russians had appointed the nazi-individualist as headmaster of the reopened

128

children's school. "It is odd," they grumbled, "that an active party member should be the first to get a job so important while none of the socialists or liberals who suffered for their opinions are rewarded. He was appointed only because he turned communist three days ago."

As I idly looked around, Ludwigsfelde was on that day almost deserted of soldiers except for a regiment of Poles in well-cut uniforms resembling those of the British. The sight of them was a relief compared to the oppression we felt at the mere sound of Russian voices, for although the Poles' language was as foreign as theirs, its tone was less loud and rough, and the expression on their faces and all their spontaneous reactions were like those of Western people. A barbaric energy emanated from Russians that did not evoke a conscious dislike, but filled the streets with the physical presence of a force so strong that it blotted out any form of vitality other than their own. As the women were starting to talk in awed whispers about the doctor's disappearance, my strength failed me. I fainted from the fatigue of standing for too long, and only recovered consciousness again at the doctor's house, where the girls had carried me.

I opened my eyes to find the doctor's wife, a blue-eyed baby in her arms, in despair. Four days ago, her husband had visited a patient in a nearby village, and since then all trace of him had gone, in spite of the eagerness of Russian authorities in Ludwigsfelde to bring him back where his services were so urgently required. The girls came to fetch me with the bread they had obtained. They brought the hopeful news that Ludwigsfelde, an important railway centre for the distribution of supplies to the capital, would in a few weeks be included in the Berlin zone governed by the four Powers and become part of the American Sector, whose border was only five miles away. "I am convinced it will happen," my husband said, and I wanted to believe him. It seemed logical, but I could not silence my private misgivings. When had anything happened in the last few years that was logical or desirable?

I was diverted from my broodings over our insecure existence by the vital necessity of finding new food supplies. Although I knew little about gardening, I felt I must make use of the neglected kitchen-garden that lay outside the park, twenty minutes walk from the house. The villagers would not help, because they were indifferent to money and only interested in the milk and butter they received in exchange for labour from peasants who owned cows, which we did not possess. Luckily three of the former Serb prisoners who had not succeeded in getting transport home, came back to Kerzendorf for a while, and as they were expert gardeners, they taught me with great patience how to sow seeds and tend the growing plants.

One day, when I returned to the house tired but happy from this absorbing occupation, I found an unexpected visitor who out of concern for us had risked herself and her bicycle on the long ride to our village. It was Lisa Tarnow, a handsome and robust woman of thirty-five, who had been our manicurist in Berlin until she had moved into a little house and garden near Kerzendorf after her marriage, when she had retained us as her only clients and come to manicure us every Sunday.

She told us how in the fighting and ensuing disorder in her village, she had frequently been raped in her lonely house, until one day she met the Russian commander who took her under his protection. They fell in love with each other, although they had no language in common, and when several months later he was ordered back to Russia, he called in an interpreter to use all his eloquence in begging Lisa to accompany him. When she replied that she could not possibly abandon her child or her husband, who was a prisoner of war, the officer ordered the interpreter to say: "Come with me, you will have other children and you will forget what lies behind you." She cared for him enough to wish to follow him to his distant country and refused him only after a long hesitation.

I found in Lisa an ally in my gardening projects, and she promised to bring me some tomato plants on the following Sunday.

The luxury of a manicure was all the more enjoyable for its outrageous contrast to the prevailing atmosphere. When I asked her to stay for lunch, I found that Ida had been so shocked at Lisa having loved a Russian, she had locked away all the food and had completely vanished herself, although it was now one o'clock and Lisa had a two hours ride before her.

That afternoon our friends from Ludwigsfelde came over to barter clothes for milk and vegetables from the farmers, and brought the strange tale of the doctor's return to his wife after a fortnight's absence.

As he was leaving a patient's house on the last evening before his disappearance, Russian officers had called to him from a passing car. They stopped, he saw them stare at him, then at each other in amazement.

"Get in at once," they ordered.

The doctor begged to be allowed to send a message to his wife, but he was peremptorily pulled into the car and whirled away. They drove on for hours until late at night they arrived at a prison camp for German prisoners where the officers were stationed.

The doctor was thrust into a bare dark room. After a while a soldier carrying a candle arrived, who stared at him with the same maddening surprise as the officers had shown, and insisted that he was a Russian deserter who was pretending not to understand Russian. The doctor showed him his papers which were in perfect order and in vain asked for an explanation. Finally, he was allowed to sleep. Next morning more men came to question him, then two officers arrived who roughly told him to follow them. He was led past many soldiers, always arousing the same inexplicable surprise, till at last he stood in an office facing the Russian commander of the camp who was bending over some papers. When he lifted his head, the doctor's mind reeled, for he was looking into a face as identical to his as if he were gazing into a mirror, at his own eyes, mouth, nose. The other's hair was cut differently, he noted with relief, so he had not lost his mind, but hands, ears and expression were exactly the same. Both men were speechless, their whole life concentrated in their eyes which they fixed on each other, until the commander got up, hugged the doctor enthusiastically and exclaimed: "God sent you to me, brother!"

From this moment the doctor was given charge of the medical supervision of the camp, and enjoyed the commander's fullest confidence. They tried to teach each other their languages and collaborated in doing their best for the men under their charge. The commander would not consent to let his friend send a word to his wife lest Ludwigsfelde should demand his return.

Early one morning, having sensed an unusual stir around him, the doctor's door opened, six men entered, marched him off and threw him into a prison cell. He found himself confined with a man condemned for a minor offence, who knowing Russian, had overheard that the commander of the camp had been denounced and arrested for his friendship with the doctor. A new commander was now in charge, to whom his predecessor's friend was so suspect, that he was to be sent off by convoy to Russia, there to disappear for ever in a concentration camp. During the confusion in the camp occasioned by the change of command, the doctor and his companion managed to climb out of the cell window and make their escape. The doctor returned at last after two long days of walking through woods and byways, still dazed by the danger of his experience.

In the evening my husband and I went into the garden where lilac and snowbells were in full flower. He must have been feeling unwell, for he walked slowly, and suddenly stood still and pointed with his stick to a secluded stretch of grass between high trees.

"I wish to be buried under those beeches," he said. "I want the grave covered by a slab of the grey local stone, cut in the style of the 1800 period, bearing my name in flowing, graceful letters." He impressed on me in minute detail the way he wished his funeral to be conducted. "Ask the clergyman to hold the

132

service in the library," he went on. "The light white and gilt panelling will keep the ceremony from being too gloomy. Place my Baroque ivory figure of Christ on the coffin, which you must not forget to cover with the large piece of red velvet." Age had conferred on the velvet many hues from ruby to dark burgundy and had worn it threadbeare, for Freddy did not care for anything new-looking, but only chose materials and carpets that bore a visible evidence of the passing of years.

He was irritated at not being certain he would retain consciousness after death, for he distrusted my efficiency and wanted to supervise arrangements from Heaven. I begged him to stop, but he was diverted by further excellent ideas that were to make the occasion memorable.

A ceremony, a dinner, a dance had for him the importance of an artistic creation. His attitude towards his guests was that of a producer to his actors or a conductor to his orchestra. Max Reinhardt called him a rival, and at one time asked him to work for the stage, but Freddy refused, for he disliked publicity. His friends were his audience. He was sensitive to their problems, ready to give practical help or startlingly unconventional but always wise advice. But at a party, everybody and everything present, including his wife, the furniture and the flowers, became part of a production that he directed with an obsession for perfection. He always made himself responsible for arranging the china and silver on the table in endless variation. He would telephone to girls and women before a dinner-party to discuss with them which of their dresses would best fit into the color scheme he had planned. A strain of melancholia in his character made him look for compensations in seeking to produce an atmosphere of beauty according to the dictates of his own taste, enlivened by the sensual pleasure of a party, and the vivid enjoyment he was the first to feel.

That day he was worried by the idea that he would be sent off to some clinic in the event of a heart seizure of which the doctor had warned him. It was a nightmare to his fastidious

133

mind to have to spend his last days in the bleak surroundings of a hospital with its sinister sounds and smells, to submit to a strict routine, eat bad food and be confined in a bare, impersonal room. He wanted to die at home, among the objects he had collected and wished to use and touch until his eyes finally closed. He made me promise solemnly not to allow a doctor to send him away from home, however ill he was. I gave him my word that I would never let this happen.

Chapter XI

BY EVENING I was always worn out. Sleep swept away my worries. I would awaken to a fresh world, a spring morning full of golden light, and have the strength to begin anew.

When at the first quiet moment Ida and I went to the spot in the garden where we had buried our little box of trinkets, we found that whole corner of the park unrecognizable. Since we had buried our treasure, tanks had driven into bushes, over-turned trees and effaced paths, and where at the beginning of April there had been no leaves, now in May, the green branches, grass and jasmine bushes carrying their rich load of flowers had transformed the scene. Should we ever find it again? In spite of our impatience we would have to put off our search. It would still be dangerous. A few days before, the army had been strictly forbidden to loot, but there were many deserters and stragglers who had lost their units and, unlike the local police, were armed so that they could menace or rob as they pleased.

I went with my husband to see what had been the fate of the eighteenth-century books that we had stored in a tool-house. We found the top of the crate broken in and the room littered with torn out pages and engravings, and bits of the green morocco leather binding of Lafontaine's *Fables* and many other books that had been ripped off with a knife. Missing volumes of a set saddened me even more than if I had lost them entirely. Their absence was as distressing as a statue without its head or a church bereft of its spire.

On our way home I gathered a large bunch of lilac, intending to place it in the library as an act of faith to prove to myself that I believed it possible to live in my own rooms again, not only to cross them furtively on my way to hiding.

As we neared the house, a figure unexpectedly detached itself from the trees. Recognizing a soldier, I quickly dropped my garden scissors into a bush before he could see them and take them away from me. He went up to Freddy, took the books from his hands and returned them to him when he found them uninteresting. He then examined our wrists for watches and found none, and next he put his hands into our pockets and turned them inside out. When at last he let us go, he insisted on accompanying us.

"I want to come with you and see your house," he said.

Monk signalled from his window for us to take refuge in his living-room, but the soldier got there just after us, and entered clamouring for cigarettes and schnapps. When his eye lighted on Monk's harmonium he sat down without another word and began to play so well that I should have stayed to listen if my husband had not made me a sign to follow him. We had just closed our front door when he began thundering on it. We let down curtains and blinds and did not dare go out while he prowled around the house all day.

One of the plundered cases had contained an eighteenth-century Nymphenburg china service, that had been collected piece by piece by my grandmother over many years. It had included plates, tureens and candlesticks on which flowers and butterflies were painted on a white background lightly touched with gold. I was told that they had been distributed in the village to be used by soldiers in billets that had since been abandoned, so I went from house to house asking for them. To my joy, I discovered some of the dishes and plates, though many had been broken and the decorative pieces thrown away as useless.

"There must be more in the mess where the soldiers are eating now," a woman said.

As my husband was too ill to get up that day, I would not have tried to retrieve them without his assistance. Was it worth while, was it not absurd to take a personal risk for a few china plates that might be stolen or lost again any day? Was it not more of a burden than a pleasure to own their fragile beauty in a world where there no longer seemed to be either use or place for them?

"Let us detach ourselves once and for all from possessions," I pleaded with Freddy. "Let us buy ourselves back by deliberately giving them up." "To renounce them without fighting is cowardly," was his answer. "To measure one's strength against alien forces is to be alive. What are games like baseball or poker but a mimicry of the same pleasure? The material value of things is irrelevant, it is the imagination and the skill of the artists' design in the knives, spoons and chairs I use that instead of depressing me by clumsy patterns, transform the drabness of existence and enchant me with their harmony. Objects daily teach me more about differences in style and quality in a secret language of imperceptible signs which I understand, as men in fairytales understood the language of animals. Had the plates irretrievably disappeared we should have to forget about them, but to abandon them voluntarily would be to give up part of myself."

Flanked by faithful Ida, I went to the building where the men were having their meal.

Standing in the doorway of the mess-hall I said, "You are eating from dishes that belonged to my grandmother and that remind me of her. Could I exchange them for these of another pattern that I have here under my arm?"

The soldiers went on noisily eating their soup, only half understanding my request, while they idly stared and acquiesced with an indifferent gesture.

The man who had harried us all when drunk the day before was one of those present in the mess. The previous night he and some others had forced their way into houses and wrecked all the furniture. I saw in his fixed expression that he had renewed his intention of following me into the house. He got up from the

137

table and followed me when I left, pushed against the front door when I tried to close it and a moment later, to Freddy's startled surprise, stood in front of him in the room and walked about slowly looking at everything in silent curiosity.

He grabbed the pen lying on the table with which my husband had been writing, rolled it about in his fingers, and put it in his pocket. Next, he pulled out a flask and invited us to drink with him. I wished to pacify him by assenting, but Freddy protested in an indignant aside:

"How can anyone be simultaneously a thief and a guest? I refuse to sit at the same table or speak to him."

When I had manœuvred the man out into the kitchen, he told me that he was a schoolteacher and was fond of playing the piano and the organ. In all the years he had been away from his distant village, the Western houses he had seen had made him dissatisfied with his own humble existence, revealing to him a higher standard of living than he had ever conceived.

"In Russia only men at the top have everything, we nothing," he said, violently striking the table. "Many others think as I do; if you repeat this, I will be shot," he continued in a lower voice, looking around. Though he knew no other system than Communism, he was a human being who suffered from the constant menace of denunciation and imprisonment; as a man of peasant stock he hated collective farming and the ever-changing agricultural laws.

The whole peasant population in a district of the province he came from, thousands of men and women who had dared protest against the new regulations, had been bundled into trucks about two o'clock one morning and deported to the other end of Russia, to a new climate, where another dialect was spoken, and set to work in quarries. The sobs and cries he had heard rang unforgettably in his ears and had filled him with lasting resentment.

Later the farmer's wife came to see me in great perturbation. "I warn you of that schoolteacher," she cried. "He is dangerous."

138

"Oh no," I said, "we parted on good terms."

It seemed that he had gone over from our house to the farmers who were milking their cows and, after standing about for some time in a moody silence, had bluntly inquired if we were land-owners. When he was answered in the affirmative, he exclaimed:

"You should kill them, they belong to a class that you must exterminate as we have done in Russia."

When the farmer explained that they had no reason for hating us, and that he himself owned more land than we did, the man left angrily for the village, where he surprised people to whom our death was of no interest at all, by trying to arouse them against us.

"He is now trying to fan up resentment against you in the soldiers' mess," the woman said.

What had gone on in his mind? He had left me with smiles, shaken me by the hand, and wished me health and happiness. Did he regret his confidence in me? Had he suddenly remembered some propaganda slogan?

"They are all like that," the farmer's wife remarked, shaking her head. "They change from friend to foe from one second to another, and become different people. It is lucky that he and his men have been ordered away tonight; who knows what he might have done."

There was a knock on the door. Could it be our enemy again? But it was Mr. Fest, back from his dangerous expedition to Berlin. We hardly dared ask him for news, fearing what we might be told. To our unbounded relief he told us that our flat was still standing, although the house was riddled with bullets and the window-panes shattered. The other buildings on the square were entirely burnt out.

A letter he brought from Hedi told us how she and old Pauline had stayed alive through the heavy bombardment that had rung in our ears with so much terror. Its effect had been incomparably less destructive than that of the bombs which had gone straight through a house to leave only its shell, while the

139

horizontal machine-gun shots did not penetrate either wall or cellars. The inhabitants lived underground for weeks, darting out during a lull in the shooting to get water at pumps at the corners of the streets. When the fighting stopped, Russians swarmed into the murky cellars and raped women with a sort of hysteria. Now Berlin had grown quiet, but there was little food. We had to read and re-read Hedi's letter before we could grasp all it conveyed.

Winterfeldt, a friend who had been imprisoned for over a year for his opposition to National-Socialism and had now been released by the Russians, had been to our flat in Berlin. He left a distressing message to tell us that Count Albrecht Bernstorff, for many years Counsellor at the German Embassy in London, who had been in the same prison, had disappeared. He had been a cultivated, gay and utterly fearless man, who from the first had opposed National-Socialism and helped its victims. One day he was sent to a concentration camp on being denounced by a widow of a relation of his, whose aim it was to get Bernstorff out of the way in order to have his country house in Mecklenburg assigned to her son. She did not succeed, for after many months of captivity Albrecht was freed with great difficulty thanks to the courageous efforts of his friends. Then again he continued to save persecuted people and openly expressed his hatred of the régime.

Whenever I saw him I implored him to be careful in what he said. "Help your friends, take part in a conspiracy, then it will be worth while being a martyr, but be careful," I begged him. "Resist repeating dangerous jokes, do not express your opinions openly, try to remain alive for the time when you will be needed. So many liberals and socialists have already been killed fighting or have died in camps that there will be no one left to serve a future that may soon be here."

He was a tall, heavy man who carried his weight lightly. His movements were rapid. I still see his blue eyes growing serious in his large young-looking face.

140

"I believe in freedom of speech no matter what the consequences are," he replied. "It is on principle that I refuse to curb my tongue." The last time we met was on the evening before his departure for Switzerland, where he went on business for the bank where he worked. We and others begged him to wait there until the end of the war, for because of his integrity and his sane judgment in foreign affairs, we all saw in him a future negotiator, ambassador or Minister of Foreign Affairs. But he answered our entreaties with: "I do not dream of running away."

In Switzerland he was spied upon and denounced for consorting with enemies of National-Socialists and on his return he was again imprisoned. After the failure of the conspiracy of July 1944, his name was found on lists of those suggested for inclusion in a future government; he was relentlessly interrogated and endured torture with unflinching courage, giving nobody and nothing away.

By April 1945, when Berlin was already half occupied by Russian troops, the prison guards, foreseeing the end of the war, began to show a new leniency to their charges that made the condemned men feel that the end of their suffering was drawing near. Only two days before all the prisoners were liberated by the Russians, SS men appeared with an order to take away Bernstorff and some others, and it now seems certain they were all shot on that day. None of them were ever heard of again, nor were their bodies found.

The silence outside was interrupted by the clamouring of hundreds of French and Italian voices demanding to see us. It was a long column of men on their way to repatriation by Allied orders, who wished to be put up in the village for one night. They were in a hurry to get away from the Russians whose behaviour to them was even more obnoxious than to the Germans.

While we were busy getting billets for them in the village, Ulla Zarn came running up in great anxiety to call me home, for a regiment of Russian soldiers had entered the park to

141

overturn the stone statues and tear up the rhododendrons like naughty children. In the middle of the lake, on a small over-grown island, stood an old bronze Buddha sent back years ago from China by a friend of my grandparents. The Russians had smashed it and thrown the pieces into the water.

"We will never get home safely," sobbed Ulla. One of the Frenchmen protested furiously, "No women shall be attacked while we are there." His friends agreed, and about a dozen of them decided to escort us back. They placed the two of us be-tween them and with set faces led us through the groups of shouting and hilarious soldiers until they delivered us safely at our door. From within the house we observed new troops of men coming and going, so we dared not venture out. After an unattractive lunch of thin soup, I started washing dishes, a task at which I fancied myself proficient, while Ida, whose conven-tions were as rigid as those of a mandarin, denounced me as an amateur. My pride was wounded, and when she shrewishly tried to pull the basin filled with water away from me, I lifted it up in a sudden fit of anger and poured it over her. Dripping from head to foot, she rushed to her room and Freddy, who had heard the commotion, came in, shocked at my behaviour. I swore never to lose my temper again. After a time Ida emerged from her room, and we all appeased each other. Soon internal calm prevailed and we passed the rest of the day patiently in a state of siege, with voices and songs surging around the walls of the house.

Next morning they had all gone, and I could return to my garden where work was an endless source of pleasure, and every effort was immediately rewarded.

When the asparagus and other vegetables began to mature, I was able to exchange them for the farmers' milk, so that we no longer felt as hungry as before. Yet all of us who lived on the same diet, though not starving, were in a continual state of weakness, our eyesight became blurred, memory failed us and other troubles set in which the doctor explained as the result of lack of meat, eggs and especially of fat.

Under the pressure of want we acquired a new attitude towards food, a caveman's perception of the minimum the body required to stay fit, and a hunter's acute instinct to procure what was essential. We had the new experience of finding that butter not only produced an effect of immediate well-being, but was a stimulant more powerful than alcohol, capable of reviving ebbing vitality.

As I was tidying the paths of a little garden laid around a sundial in front of the house, and trimming the box-hedges with my shears, a low voice called my name. A woman approached, dressed like a peasant in a long skirt with a shawl over her head. I recognized her as Baroness Lowen, the country neighbour who had offered to take me West with her some weeks ago. Having fled from Lowen shortly before the Russian invasion, she had now walked back to see if it were possible to regain possession of her house and estate. Just before entering Lowen a peasant had prevented her from going any further with the earnest warning that a Russian warrant had been issued for her arrest on the grounds that she was the mother of an officer and belonged to a Junker family. She had come to us for a rest, in great distress at her realization that she would have to give up Lowen for ever. She was convinced of her danger, and the next day left to return to the West. Her news filled me with alarm, but my husband's reaction was: "You see how right we were not to go away from Kerzendorf; one has no title to what one wilfully abandons."

In the afternoon the clergyman came to visit us on his way back from Berlin, where he had gone to look up his father, a publisher sixty-five years old. He had found him alive, but his printing press, reserves of paper and books had gone up in flames. Yet he had not complained, and thought only of rebuilding his business as quickly as possible. On all sides one met a tireless resourcefulness and the same energy that in a misguided form had created the destruction surrounding us, was now being used to repair what had been needlessly destroyed.

143

In a newspaper, miraculously new to us as it was only three days old, the clergyman showed us a report of Himmler's death, and articles about life in other cities and countries. Slowly the outside world was becoming visible again through a haze, as when clouds disperse after heavy rains. The gentleness of life was being re-established elsewhere. Were we alone cut off from it?

The clergyman laughingly dived into the leg of his high leather boot and got out a wrist-watch. He told us that on his way back from Berlin a Russian had been so attracted by his boots that he had ordered him to take them off and hand them over. When he had pulled the left one off, the Russian could not stamp his big foot into it, and the clergyman had the luck to walk on in them, his watch undiscovered.

He consulted it and shook his head:

"The Catholic priest was to meet me here at five o'clock," he said; "now it is seven, and there is no sign of him. If I wait any longer my wife will be worried."

After a time the priest appeared and asked to be excused for coming too early. It turned out that while we had been told to set the clock forward for summer time, the priest's local commander had ordered it to be put back three hours, so that when for him it was five o'clock in the afternoon, for us the evening had begun and elsewhere time had not changed at all, because Russian officers had been convinced that cows liked to be woken and milked at their usual hour. So appointments between nearby places never came off, and the inhabitants were as widely separated from each other by living in different portions of the day as if divided by an ocean in different parts of the globe.

When a little later I went to visit Businsky and his wife, who looked as round and fat as Tweedledum and Tweedledee, I was surprised to see a photograph of Stalin standing on the counter.

"Russians buy here, you know," Businsky said apologetically, and then asked me to enter his back room for a talk.

"When are the Americans coming to replace the Russians?"

144

he asked me. "If they don't arrive soon I shall find myself obliged to join the Communist party, for I am not interested in theories, I just want my shop to function. I can obtain the car I need to fetch supplies by permission of Russian customers who grant it only if I am a party member. If the Russian occupation continues, I strongly advise your husband to follow my example and put himself under their protection. Then he, the mayor and I could manage the affairs of the village together."

His implications of a new totalitarian system taking the place of the first worried me. Yet did not everybody else believe that the Russian troops would soon move away?

On Whit Sunday we woke to a quiet holiday, and a deserted farmyard. I was ill and in pain, and had to lie prostrate on the library sofa. Sun streamed into the peaceful room where Freddy sat writing while Bibi lay next to me. I tried to make each hour of the day as full and rich as possible and not to give way to impatience.

I was interrupted by a rude hammering on the front door, and four Russians walked in. As the day was cool, logs were burning in the grate and the soldiers backed out in alarm, for they had never seen an open fire and believed the flames were beginning to devour the house. They had come to search for weapons and looked high and low for two hours. They searched in vain, except for an unpleasant moment when they came upon a sword that had been part of Freddy's diplomatic dress. They left at last having requisitioned whatever else they fancied, but without having even glanced at the Zarns' or the refugees' rooms on the same floor, which for all they knew might have concealed all the weapons in the world.

Their visit was clearly the result of a denunciation directed specifically against us, so that we were confronted by a deliberate act of hostility which was in sharp contrast to impersonal accidents of war and defeat. We were menaced by an obscure threat, of which we did not know the origin.

I felt my heart grow cold.

Chapter XII

As I was standing in front of our house late one afternoon, a car full of soldiers drove into the farmyard. Out of it tumbled the Russian schoolteacher like a half absurd, half sinister clown in a circus. In his whining tones which we had hoped never to hear again, he asked me for a suit with a striped yellow vest, an old servant's livery he had forgotten to take while looting the cellar a few weeks ago. "I've dreamed of it every night since I saw it," he moaned.

The other soldiers laughed when I gave him what he wanted and they all went over to the farmer's house to exchange tobacco for eggs.

A little later there was a light tap on my window. Gabriel had sent his little sister to warn us he had overheard the men saying that the schoolteacher had told them of a number of women living in the farmer's and in our house, and had shown them the way to Kerzendorf. Some of the girls went off at once on hearing the news to hide in the loft of the barn. As the strangers had gone to smoke and play chess in Monk's front room, I found myself cut off from my usual retreat. "They do not seem dangerous," whispered Frau Monk; "you will be safe at home tonight."

Towards midnight I woke up to strident cries for help. I had hardly lighted my candle when Ida appeared in a state of terror mixed with triumphant satisfaction at bringing really stirring news.

"Soldiers have broken into the house," she announced in tense excitement. "They are already in the passage. We can only get away by jumping out of the window."

146

There was no time to dress. We clambered out onto the window-sill, placed our bare feet first in one, then into another of the cool and rough ridges of the wall. I slipped and fell into a soft flower bed. For a second the fresh smell of earth was the only reality, then, dazed and covered with dust, I was picked up by Ida and dragged into hiding in the shadow of the trees. The screams began again, we heard the sound of argument, and at last came the rumbling of a car driving off. Soon there was nothing but the wind rustling in the leaves.

The men had forced their way into the farmer's house with pistols in their hands, and had flashed their torchlights into the faces of sleeping women. They overpowered the farmer's handsome daughter-in-law, a woman of delicate nerves whose husband was now a prisoner of war in Russia, and who had as yet managed to escape violence. Gabriel's mother had been able to protect her little maid, a young girl still sick from the results of a former raping. Being able to speak the soldiers' language they could remonstrate with them, but it was in vain that Gabriel asked, when they prepared to storm over to our house: "Why don't you go to the village where you will find girls ready to accept you?"

One of them answered in disgust, "Willing women are unclean."

Our nerves were on edge. None of us slept that night. As I came out of my room the next morning, I was startled to find myself confronted by a large group of soldiers, who had come to tell us that they had discovered an old-fashioned safe in searching the ruins of our bombed house, which they were certain concealed treasures. They had found it impossible to force its lock open, and since they refused to believe it was empty, they had dragged it to our doorstep and threatened to blow it up with a hand grenade unless I opened it for them at once. In my fright, I offered it as a present to them, begging them to set off their explosives elsewhere. We were arguing when Freddy, who had heard voices, burst in violently.

147

"Will you please tell your companion to leave my window immediately?" he called out at them. Two of them ran out and returned holding a sheepish-looking soldier.

"I was reading quietly," Freddy explained indignantly, "when this man's head was thrust inside the open window. He was brandishing a loaded pistol and rudely demanded a watch. I understand his needing one," Freddy went on in a loud tone, as if he could make his language clearer to foreigners, "for it must be tiresome not to know the time, but he must be told it is intolerable to frighten people by suddenly confronting them in this way. It might easily have given me a heart attack."

My husband's anger disturbed the men, even though they could not understand what he was saying. They shook their heads and rattled off on their cart, weighed down by the heavy safe.

For a while my husband, Monk and I busied ourselves in trying to repair the door by nailing planks across it. Freddy, who was far from well, and could not bear to see any more people on that day, was about to lie down when we heard more knocks. As he let down the shutters, I stood next to him trembling, and listened to a loud pounding on the other door and on the windows. Peering out carefully, I saw what had sounded like several people was only a single but very determined man. I managed to signal to one of the passing children to fetch the Ukrainian and ask her to find out what he wanted, for he was furiously kicking at the newly repaired front door with heavy boots. When she arrived, he explained to her in a loud, hoarse voice that he was no robber, but was so anxious to see the inside of the house that he would smash doors and windows to obtain his end.

My husband said, "Since the armistice no soldier has a right to enter a house unless he has a special order, which this man has not produced."

But what if the door were broken again, leaving it open to all passers-by? So Freddy unwillingly let him in, explaining his

148

delay by saying that he had been ill in bed. The man smiled all over, pleased at his success, and stared at everything in rapt attention.

When he saw the eighteenth-century chairs with their slightly torn old silk covering, he shook his head. "Sad," he said. Then he went through to the Zarns' apartment where he preferred the furniture covered with bright material and reached out his hands towards some spoons that were on a table.

"Don't take anything from us," Mrs. Zarn besought him. "We are *robota*" (workers)—it was one of the words we all had learned.

"A worker like me?" he said incredulously, looking around at what was to him as sumptuous as a palace.

"Yes, yes," she insisted.

There was a silence; then he put the spoons back and sighed deeply.

"Poor Russia, we also would like to have water coming out of the wall, light shining from the ceiling," he pointed towards the chandelier, "and not live in the same room with pigs and chicken."

He returned to the library, sat down, slapped his thigh contentedly, and declared that he found the room pleasant and our company so new and interesting, that he proposed to spend several days with us to study our mode of existence. While Freddy went out for a moment to fetch the local policeman, the soldier pulled out volumes from the bookcases, rummaged through the shelves and attempted to conceal something in his pocket.

After the police had persuaded our visitor to return to his billet, my husband put his hand behind *Keats' Poems*, where he kept his last precious little bottle of a French hair lotion, Houbigant's 'Eau de Violettes', and found to his consternation that it had gone. It was a blow, for in the confusion in which we were living, not only strict necessities counted. It was not the important losses alone which moved us. A small luxury such as a

149

scent with its power of evocation brought us, who were caught in a rough present, a reassurance of our own identity which we were fast losing.

But as the magic liquid was nowhere to be found, we went after the soldier and urgently begged him to return it, explaining that it was not vodka. Too late, he had already swallowed it at one gulp.

"It was the best drink I've ever tasted," he remarked happily, wiping his lips with the back of his hand and exhaling a strong odour of hair-lotion.

In the afternoon, when a few officers accompanied by Russian girls came to picnic in the park, one of the men who entered the house to borrow glasses was shocked to see the wreckage. He sat down, asked me to drink with him and said, after looking around carefully to be sure that no one was listening: "War is mankind's greatest misfortune. Years of fighting as well as the conquest of a foreign country demoralizes boys. But how could anything result from political systems led either by Hitler or by Stalin?" He spoke in a voice hard with hatred and expectorated at the mention of the two names.

"Could not your system change?" I asked.

"Oh no," he answered, and jerked his head towards the window. He shrugged his shoulders: "It is the will of God," and he tossed down a big glass of spirits. He advised me to tell everyone in the house to call out loudly for help in case of further intrusions, for as soldiers were being strictly punished for disorder, they would not dare risk detection.

When I told him of my pride in the strawberries that were coming up and complained that the soldiers were at that very moment crushing and ruining the beds, he offered to drive them away if I accompanied him to gather a basket of fruit for him. We went to the garden together and he cursed the soldiers in ringing tones that sent them scuttling off in all directions, leaving me to go on with my work.

No incident could interrupt my passionate preoccupation

150

with the success or failure of what I was trying to grow. I went out in the dewy freshness of each morning to seek the companionship of plants and to respond to their tacit demand for care which was as strong on troubled days as on quiet ones. My mind concentrated on their needs, on trying to learn what they required. I now had help from village women, whom I paid partly in money and partly in the vegetables we had brought to life together. They were pleased by my working as long or longer than they did, for they saw in it the proof of our attachment to Kerzendorf and our refusal to abandon it or them for greater security elsewhere.

One of the women told me of her great distress at having lost her husband during the last weeks of fighting. All his comrades excepting himself had worn civilian suits under their uniforms so they could escape more easily, and when he tried to get away from the hopeless battle in the streets of Berlin, an SS man who was watching the soldiers had shot him in the nape of the neck.

We were just going off to lunch when some children came running up.

"Go home," they cried. "The Russian commander of the district has just telephoned to the Mayor of Kerzendorf to notify him that several regiments of Mongols, thousands of men, are coming through here on their way back east. They sweep women, children and cattle along with them on their march and shoot down whoever opposes them. Anyone who values his safety must keep away from the streets and highway and go into hiding at once."

We went cold with fear and at once hastened home. As I was late, my husband had already begun his luncheon and he was cross at my having kept him waiting.

"Sit down and eat," he insisted. "Talk afterwards."

I explained. He would not listen.

"That sort of thing does not happen. Eat."

Finally, he was impressed by Ida's and my nervousness and

sent Monk to question the Mayor. He returned to tell us that the Mayor as well as the whole village was in a state of panic, everyone had disappeared, scattering into the woods and fields, hiding wherever they could.

"Go off singly, to be less conspicuous," was the advice given.

The Russian officer was going to telephone again as soon as the hordes reached his town; two Kerzendorf men were posted at the entrance to the village and were ordered to blow the trumpet three times, as a signal of the Mongols' approach. The most alarming feature of the situation was the helplessness and anxiety of the Russian authorities themselves.

Ida and the others had already vanished.

"You will be ill again if you go without your meals," said Freddy in a warning tone, "but I will not keep you."

I quickly picked up a golden thimble, a nail file, scissors and a detective novel which I had just begun, all the belongings that were most important to me at the moment. The hiding-place I chose was an empty space well concealed between a wall and some bushes surrounding an eighteenth-century statue in grey sandstone of a scantily clad girl holding up a lyre in a pose of pleasing affectation.

I lay down on the grass, but hard as I strained my ears, I heard nothing but familiar garden sounds. After a while I began to read. Then, unmistakably, the silence was shattered by an ominous bugle sounding one, two, three blasts that made my blood freeze despite the warm day. Silence closed in again and remained unbroken by steps or voices. I tried to go on with my book, but the solution to the young heiress' murder seemed tame in comparison with today's events. There was a cosiness about a masked man slinking into a comfortable block of flats to kill a girl which made me feel slightly superior that afternoon. I began to get hungrier every minute, and curious to know what was happening.

A mosquito settled on me, the next instant another, then more, oh! many more. Word had been given of my presence.

They arrived in buzzing swarms, danced around me in groups and started to sting. When I tried to drive them off by catching one or two, a hundred attacked me, until my hiding-place in the garden became so intolerable that I could stand it no longer. I thought of the ten thousand Mongols and quailed, but it was a choice between a reality and a possibility. Barbaric hordes were on their way to drag me along and to annihilate me, but meanwhile savage insects drank my very blood. I set my teeth, got up and warily slipped along the wall. The farmyard was abandoned, a lonely piece of paper flapped in the dust, not a soul was to be seen. I looked into the library where Freddy sat quietly writing.

"Do sit down," he said. "How can you be such a coward?"

I went to the Monks' empty rooms, and anxiously waited for an eternity until at one moment the uncanny silence was interrupted by a far-away singing of many husky voices. As they became louder, a boy came running from the village. Masses of Mongols had reached the cross-roads, but had then chosen to take the by-pass going around the village, just as the fighting troops had done some weeks before. By a miraculous good fortune we had escaped.

After a long time the villagers returned, relating gruesome stories of raping and brutality that had occurred in less fortunate villages. We were all of us at the end of our tether; no one worked any more that afternoon.

In the next few days we heard the steady rolling of trucks moving along the highroad transporting Poles, Serbs, Bulgarians back to their countries. The repatriation of the countless prisoners and workers was well organized and aided by their own impatience to get home. Would they rediscover what they had so longed for during these last years? They not only expected to see a house and a family, but to come back to their own lost youth, to conditions that had changed as much as themselves while they had been away.

Once a row of cars bearing hundreds of Dutchmen who had

153

driven through Buckow on their way from Eastern Germany to Holland made a short halt in Kerzendorf, and brought news of my sister-in-law's house. When Russian troops had approached the village, the Nazi mayor had ordered it to be blown up so that it should not be of any use either to Germans or to the enemy after defeat. The old walls, the baroque ceilings with their riot of white stucco, in an enchanting variety of emblems, scrolls, fruit and flying cherubs, had been destroyed in an act of senseless vandalism, for the house had no military value whatsoever.

During our conversation, one of the Dutchmen mentioned casually that Kerzendorf would become part of the Russian zone of occupation. The words sounded like a death-knell in my ears, but another man hotly contradicted him, saying that he had heard on the wireless the day before that an independent state would be constituted between the Oder and Elbe, and that the province of Brandenburg would be included in the Four-Power Zone of Berlin.

Freddy gave me courage by accepting this as the only possible truth and refusing to consider any other possibility.

He would not listen to my fears. I foresaw an endless denial of a normal, everyday life if the Russians did not leave, for although as yet we had experienced no official curtailment of liberty as under the Nazis, and disorder was now being punished, we had no natural allies amongst the population. We were mutually attached to each other, but the uneducated peasants were without influence and lacking in any sense of political responsibility. People like ourselves, landowners and middle class, had all fled; those that had remained were fast joining the Communist Party to safeguard their interests, and expected us to do the same. What enmities would be aroused when one day they realized that nothing could make us follow their example? Freddy impressed on me that it was our duty to play our part here. But what could our place, our usefulness be in a world where we were backed by no one and completely isolated?

154

"We have been right in taking the risk to stay," Freddy answered. "For we were not killed in battle and succeeded by our presence in keeping the house and part of our possessions, which would have been irretrievably lost if we had left them to their fate. We must persist in our loyalty to what surrounds us and wait patiently until the wave of Russian and local Communism, so foreign to Europe, has had time to recede."

Among the daily arrivals of people of all nationalities who violated the place with their strange views and unaccustomed personalities was a familiar visitor whom we received with soothing regularity. It was Louise Radinsky, the masseuse, whose offices were necessary to my husband's health. She was a handsome girl who braved the dangers of the road to come over on foot from a pleasant bungalow she owned in Ludwigsfelde, where she lived with a little daughter of six, an illegitimate child whom she brought up with primness and severity. "I do not want her to behave as I did," she remarked. Yet no social stigma was attached either to her or to the child, and many men had wished to marry the good-looking girl who earned a comfortable living. Illegitimacy had been encouraged by the Nazis to enlarge the population, but apart from the official view, a reaction against strict Victorian morality had developed in all classes of the country even in small towns. It was an attitude that went back to the seventeenth and eighteenth centuries, when errors were not recommended, but more easily excused than during the reign of unbending nineteenth-century convention.

She had managed with difficulty to elude all Russian advances, especially those of an officer whom she met in the hospital where she worked and who pursued her with his attentions. One day he happened to pass by just as an ordinary soldier was trying to engage her in conversation. Her admirer unfastened the pistol from his hip, took aim and shot the man through the head, so that he fell at her feet lifeless, leaving the girl to run away terrorized by such excessive chivalry.

155

She was with us when the Mayor arrived with excellent news. He had talked to the Russian district commander about my husband and myself, and had brought us a paper written and signed in Russian on one side and by the Mayor on the other, certifying that we were under the protection of them both and in case of danger were to apply to the Mayor to telephone to the Commander. He was giving us a life-line that removed the disquieting feeling that we were an alien element in the community. Yet although I should have been reassured, as there seemed to be nothing more to fear, I remained suspicious and on my guard.

While Freddy went on writing, I started to sort out some picture postcards of paintings. Among them, Claude Lorrain's 'The Enchanted Palace', a landscape with high trees half concealing a palace in the background, wrung my heart by its lovely calm and satisfied my overwhelming need for peace. I let fall all the others to drink in every particle of this photograph. It was this picture with its long serene lines that I always kept with me in the months to come.

Chapter XIII

WE LIVED on in complete insecurity, in a continual strain of trying to guess at our future while depending on people whose mentality we understood even less than their language.

As the Kerzendorf men were now employed in dismantling railroad equipment that was to be sent to Russia, we were at the mercy of the thousands of Ukrainians who were passing through daily. It was dangerous to go out except in groups, for they robbed and stripped solitary wanderers. German police were only allowed to carry big bludgeons, so that they could not control armed vagrants, savage from despair at being treated as outlaws by their own countrymen. The Ukraine's hostile attitude towards the administrative centralization in Moscow and its reaction against communist doctrines had resulted in deeply rooted mutual antagonism. The Ukrainians knew they would not be taken home to the Ukraine, but that they were on their way to Siberia or to work in the Ural mines, and so used every occasion to escape from their guards and convoys.

One quiet summer afternoon we were startled by a sudden peal of bells. People came running up from all sides, calling out that a large band of Ukrainians were just about to attack Kerzendorf. From the window I could see some of them breaking into the farmer's house and dragging out sheep. One had a goose under his arm, others had an armful of hens, and a man who was carrying Mrs. Zarn's rabbits by their long silky ears, turned and, as he noticed Monk watching him from his doorstep, started to insult him; his companions joined in, but the bells were louder than their voices. We could only see their lips moving.

157

Two trucks drove up, filled with men and women warning the marauders in a pantomime of gestures to take flight before they were caught. The trucks then picked up men and animals and drove off at a furious pace, leaving us dumbfounded at the brief scene we had witnessed.

Once, just as my husband had arrived in the kitchen-garden to fetch me in to lunch, seven Ukrainians leaped over the fence and began swarming over the garden beds. They were fascinated by the sight of onions, but as there were only a few left, they flew into a rage and in their anger pulled out flowers and vegetables by their roots, trampled on them, broke branches, spoiled the straight lines of beds and paths with their big boots, and would not listen to my husband when he reasoned with them. Ida ran towards the village, blowing shrilly on her whistle, Bibi bravely acted the part of a watchdog and barked indignantly at the top of her lungs. Police arrived with their cudgels, followed by stray Russian soldiers, delighted to join in the fun of driving away the intruders. They came none too soon, for the Ukrainians had begun to threaten to take away our clothes and shoes. When they had fled, and were but running figures on the horizon, the soldiers, who saw how afraid we were, took little cakes out of their pockets and good-naturedly offered them to us.

Everyone's nerves became frayed from nights constantly interrupted by the battering on doors. It was easier to keep one's self-control in daylight, but even then every moment was mixed with dread. To give up gardening would have been a relief, for it was a strain to go out knowing what we should have to face, but I could not expect the women who were just as frightened as myself to work for me while I stayed safely at home.

One of them had lately arrived from Silesia, the province taken over by Poland some weeks earlier, where Germans were now being treated exactly as they had formerly behaved towards the Poles. They denied their enemies' children education in schools and universities, forbade them to ride in trains or buses and made them undergo the identical humiliations they themselves had been made to suffer. This woman and many others had been evicted from her village when it became Polish, as Poles had once been thrown out of their homes by Germans. They were driven off on foot, abandoning house and possessions to the new owners. It was human to seek satisfaction in revenge, but, as it happened, the real culprits had escaped and those who were made to bear the burden of retaliation were innocent of any crimes. The Silesians burned with indignation at what they considered unjust treatment, and in turn developed a longing for revenge. So it would go on in an unending, senseless circle of hostility always nurtured anew between the two neighbouring countries.

The Serbs, our protectors, having taken leave of us, happy to return at last to their families in Jugo-Slavia, came back dejectedly twelve hours later. They had with great difficulty boarded a train so crowded that they had been obliged to climb through the windows into the closely packed compartments. People were travelling back home, or in search of food and things to barter. Fifty or sixty men and women sat at the risk of their lives on the roof of each carriage in constant danger of being brushed off at a tunnel or electrocuted by overhead wires. Others hung for hours on to window-sills from the outside.

While the train was waiting for the engine to be refuelled, bandits attacked it from all sides and forced the passengers to surrender their belongings at the point of machine-guns, while the intervening police were warded off by stones and shots.

The Serbs were walking down the road back towards Kerzendorf in bitter disappointment, when they found it blocked by about thirty German prisoners in civilian clothes, surrounded by several guards who were discussing the attempted flight of one of the men. He had been recaptured and brought back into line with his companions. He had not been ill-treated. "Poor fellow, he was right to try," a guard said, shrugging his shoulders. But now three other prisoners had vanished without leaving a trace, to the soldiers' serious perturbation, for they were certain to be executed if they did not deliver the right number of men.

The whole column was made to stand still. The guards scratched their heads, counted, recounted their charges, and abused each other. Gazing around helplessly their eyes fell on three of the Serbs who were looking on with interest. "We are saved!" they cried, and collaring them with great relief, pushed them forward into the group in place of the fugitives. As the Serbs spoke fluent Russian, they protested vehemently and threatened to complain to a Russian officer if they were not released at once. Anxious deliberation began again. A few yards away peasants were peacefully working in the fields. The guards rounded them up, selected three of them at random, made them fill up the column, and marched their surprised victims off to an unknown destination. There was no chance of return for them, for they had no means of explaining the error, nor would anyone be interested in their plight. Human beings were treated as ingredients in a chemical process, with an Asiatic indifference which was foreign to Europeans. To Russians, whom victory had hurled here from a distant continent, life was synonymous with constraint without appeal, with misfortune that should be accepted with unquestioning resignation. Kindness and compassion existed only outside of reality as an abstract conception.

We could now hear the news once again on a small wireless set, and one day it brought us the news of the atom bomb, Hiroshima, and peace with Japan, although we only learned the bare facts. The more explicit American station, Rias, was made inaudible by interference from the Russian station. We were again deluged with propaganda broadcast in vulgar, grating tones, and cut off from all but party indoctrination, for the Russian licensed press was written in the same irritatingly aggressive spirit as the defunct Nazi papers. Yet our ideal of

160

moral freedom became so clearly defined under this pressure, that those who doubted its realization during their own brief span of life, instilled it into the young, who in their turn were determined to hand it on intact, in a hope that their convictions would eventually pave the way to a new Renaissance.

I escaped reality for a time by developing a temperature that took me into a world of happy illusions, and I returned from it only slowly and regretfully. The rose next to my bed, the arm of a chair, the corner of a frame fixed my attention for so long that imagination curled around them, changed their outline and pattern into a face, a mountain, an animal. There was no need for action or thought, but time to concentrate on the immediate present and to live intensely.

On the July morning when I regained consciousness, the air was cool and I shivered in my room, although a fire was burning. From where I lay I saw the vividly green tops of trees and vaguely followed what went on next door through a haze of exhaustion. Villagers were going in and out of the library, calling on my husband to ask for advice about their problems. I heard Freddy's voice: "So you are the wife of the new policeman. What can I do for you? What is this large potato sack you are carrying?"

A nervous reply came: "Will you take it, please? It contains all I took from your house the evening before you returned from Ludwigsfelde. Now that my husband has an official position it compromises us to keep things belonging to you. We might be denounced for it at any minute, and he would lose his job."

I heard her get up. Freddy seemed to be as embarrassed as she was.

"I am sorry," she blurted out.

For a time I heard nothing until I woke to the voice of a man who was urgently begging my husband to sign a statement certifying that he had never belonged to the Nazi party.

"But I thought you were a member once?"

"Oh yes," said the man, "as a matter of fact, I was. But I am able to prove that at the same time my wife and I remained convinced Freemasons."

Now someone entered in great excitement to interrupt the conversation by asking to see my husband alone. It was the doctor, I realized, and he breathlessly blurted out that he had hastened over from Ludwigsfelde to convey the most wonderful news. "Halle, Erfurt and Leipzig have been taken over by Russia," he announced. "But Ludwigsfelde and Kerzendorf are now certain to be part of the four-power government of the capital and in the American Zone."

The hope of recovering a basic form of security surged up wildly within me. Was the doctor telling the truth, or were his words simply the crystallization of my own passionate wish? Would we ever again hang up clothes instead of hiding them, leave scissors or a comb on a table without their being grabbed by the first passer-by, cease to feel towards anything we used or needed as a harassed sheepdog towards straying sheep? I closed my eyes, trying to harden myself against disappointment.

A little later Freddy came in and urged me to look towards the window on my right. Through a mounting mist of fever I watched a play being enacted in front of our house by school-children, girls and boys from seven to ten years of age, to an audience of villagers sitting on benches placed on the lawn. It told the story of a great drought. A little girl implored a rural Goddess to bring rain to a parched countryside, while the other children sang and danced. One could see how absorbed they all were in the performance, so concentrated on reciting the lines, that they had forgotten about being hungry or upset by what went on around them. At the end, the teacher-Goddess, a tall fair girl, graciously granted the request in flowing verse. Her last words coincided with the falling of big drops from the sky. A moment later a heavy shower came down like a curtain, behind which grown-ups and the little actors scattered and ran for shelter. Darkness came in a loud rhythmical drumming of rain, while a large soft wave swept me away to restful shadows.

162

Chapter XIV

GERMAN SOLDIERS had returned to Kerzendorf and once more took their place in the little community. Amongst them was Frau Zarn's husband, Rudolf, formerly my parents' and later our own man-servant, who had fought in Berlin, near the Friedrichshain, the large air-raid shelter used for storing part of the Berlin Museum collections since 1939. When the building could no longer be held against the Russians, the SS threw flaming torches into it rather than let it fall into enemy hands. Unique Renaissance bronzes, brought together at the beginning of this century by Bode, the director of the Imperial Museums, rare Oriental carpets, stained glass from cathedral windows—all went up in flames.

To escape from fire and pursuit in the streets, where they were fighting for every bridge and every house, Rudolf and some companions fled down the underground passage of a subway, bullets following them into the dark. As the pipes burst, a gush of water rapidly mounted to their knees, their waists and finally their necks, and they had to resort to swimming. It was thus, instead of riding in a train, which had seemed the only possible method before this strange day, that they reached the well-known station entrance and gave themselves up as prisoners. After his release, coming through the town of Lichterfelde on his way home, Rudolf saw SS men deliberately set fire to a row of intact houses. Their purpose was to prevent Russian troops from finding shelter, but as a result their own compatriots were made homeless only a few hours before the end of the war, while Russian soldiers were comfortably installed in barracks.

The repatriated men were fully occupied in bringing in the harvest which was essential if we were not to starve in the coming winter. When the golden sheaves stood among the stubble of the fields, the Russian authorities were asked to grant our village the electricity needed to set the threshing machines in action. There was a moment of terrible doubt, then permission was given, and from then on a busy, warm humming formed the background of our days.

"The wheat becomes flour that will be your bread," it sang. The steady droning brought the priceless gift of light in its wake. Lamps came alive again, so that when dusk fell, we could read and were no longer a prey to brooding. Night lost much of its terrors since we could banish darkness at the slightest sound.

Each of us had now become the member of a hive profiting from nature's summer growth, and like bees, we stored as much as we could against the winter. Ida and I and village women obtained some jars by complicated methods of bartering, and stood in the sunny garden for long pleasant hours eating as well as picking raspberries or cherries which we later mixed with our precious supplies of sugar and carefully bottled. As fat was still very difficult to obtain, our joy was great when a peasant's wife gave me a large pitcher of unskimmed milk to make butter. It was an offence punishable by imprisonment for her to bring it as it was for me to accept it, for all milk was taken by strict regulations to a collecting centre. Here it was supposed to be distributed to the population, but it never was. It always disappeared and found its way to the black market. The woman lent me a large glass resembling a cocktail shaker, into which the milk was poured and firmly shaken, and in a few minutes the thin white liquid was surprisingly transformed into a solid golden mass of butter. The magic instrument's inventor had named it 'Columbus', because with justifiable pride he had deemed it an innovation of an importance equal to the discovery of a new continent.

164

A regulation forced bakers to close their bakeries and flour was to be distributed generally for everyone to bake their own bread. Women over seventy, who were our teachers in an art none of us had learned, brought out ancient wood vessels of a beautiful, simple design, in which we mixed leaven before forming it with our hands. We worked the whole day, to the musical accompaniment of the machine.

About that time I was woken up in the middle of one August night by a terrific explosion. I leaped out of bed and mechanically pulled on my clothes in the dark, to be ready for any eventuality. I had the door-knob in my hand when I saw lightning cut through the black sky, and realized with overwhelming relief that neither bombs nor guns but a crash of thunder had forced me awake. I returned to bed leisurely, to lie awake for a long time listening to the softly falling rain, consciously enjoying the fresh experience of physical safety.

Fresh tribulations came in the form of new groups of refugees, who instead of passing through Kerzendorf on their way West to join relatives and lodging temporarily in barns for a day or two, could not be sent on because they had nowhere to go. Orders were issued for every village to accept a certain number of them, until Kerzendorf's population swelled from 300 to over 1000, to the bitter resentment of the villagers, who saw themselves compelled to divide their scanty food supply with people coming from a part of the country so different in climate, historical background and customs, that they regarded them as foreigners. Every mouthful of food was grudged to the newcomers and they were treated with contempt, as if their homelessness were their own fault. Permanent rooms had to be assigned to them, and as they took part in the inhabitants' family life, growing irritation at this forced intimacy strained relationships still further.

The unfortunate people reacted by growing envious of their hosts, who were still in possession of what they themselves had lost, and they sought to reassure themselves by boasting about

165

their former existence in terms that regret made even more glamorous. A family of Sudeten-Germans, turned out of Czecho-Slovakia in retaliation for the Nazi treatment of the Czechs, were filled with patriotic loyalty towards their country, in spite of their eviction from it. Their attachment was not diminished, nor their admiration for Benes lessened, because an impersonal bureaucracy had treated them as enemies. When they sat around in the evening, they reminisced about the places where they had spent their entire lives and sang Czech folksongs to bring back the memory of what they had lost. One woman was so homesick that no entreaties could make her get up or touch food. She lay on her bed, her eyes shut in a despairing resolve to die.

Other refugees demanded more and more without ever being satisfied. They tried to fight destiny in blind hatred, not caring if they hurt others as they had themselves been hurt. In their ingratitude toward their benefactors they would have taken everything from them and often did not stop at theft or denunciation.

When the clergyman reminded the peasants in a sermon one Sunday that "Circumstances might have made you into refugees as well as them, yet you treat them as inferior beings," sobs came from people who found themselves understood and defended. The reproved were visibly impressed, but spiteful looks darting backwards and forwards showed that none would mend their ways. Another Sunday the clergyman began his sermon by saying that since the organ had been burned during the war, musical accompaniment was sorely needed for the church ceremonies.

"A Russian officer," he went on, "in possession of a harmonium, has offered to exchange it for a portable gramophone. If an owner of such an instrument is present and has the generosity to give it up in favour of the community, let him come to me after church."

A heated discussion started at the far end of the hall between

166

a married couple. The man got up while his wife audibly scolded him, and answered the preacher by sounds made incoherent by a mixture of decision and embarrassment. "You own such an instrument, my son," said the man from the pulpit, "and have decided to make us all a present of it for the sake of music? How can we thank you enough?" The man went purple in his effort to explain, until he finally got out that he did not care about the harmonium at all, but that he was willing to exchange his gramophone in case the Russian gentleman had a lamb to give him in return.

When the clergyman had silenced him with great difficulty, we were again diverted by the ostentatious arrival of Businsky and his wife, both dressed in dignified black, and whose attendance at church was surprisingly inconsistent with their new conversion to communism. As he settled down next to me with great ceremony, he murmured behind his hand with a significant look: "Americans are expected here very soon; they are religiously minded people," by which he meant to explain his and his wife's presence. "I have bought some English books to prepare for their arrival," he continued pompously, while a hymn was being sung, "a very interesting work of an anti-totalitarian tendency, so I was told. I have placed it in my shop-window for Americans to see immediately they arrive in the village."

I went past the store on my way home, curious to learn the title of the volumes he was displaying. I found them to be an English translation of a detailed treatise on sexual aberrations by the German doctor Magnus Hirschfeld.

The postal service was not yet functioning, but we had been accustomed for years to receiving letters without its help. Passing them on from hand to hand was an important service that friends rendered each other in an effort to elude the censorship of dangerous spies in post-offices who threw a net of suspicion over any, even the most harmless, correspondence. We had learned never to inquire who had delivered them, so we asked no question when one day two letters lay on the hall floor, where they had been pushed from underneath the closed door. We opened them eagerly.

One letter was from Charles, the lawyer with whom we had endlessly discussed the question of our staying in Kerzendorf or of taking flight. He was the only one of our acquaintances who like ourselves had taken the risk of staying in the neighbourhood of Berlin, because his parents had refused to abandon their home near Potsdam and he would not desert them. Charles' father had been no Nazi, his son had plotted against the régime, and his daughter had been sent to a concentration camp. His reason for feeling safe was that he had attended the Congress of Iranian Art in Moscow in 1935, and as a visible proof of his cordial reception he had brought back a large photo of himself and Molotov which he placed in the drawing-room. But none of this had served to protect him from the indifferent waves of war and conquest: Russian soldiers raped his daughter who had just returned from her camp, and took his priceless Oriental manuscripts and threw them into the woods like discarded toys, where they lay soaked with rain and ruined. The shock of events had broken the old man, so that he died of grief a few days later.

"I am leaving our house with my whole family," Charles went on, "because none of us feels safe in the Russian Zone."

"Nonsense," Freddy interrupted.

"The shortage of food in Berlin," Charles continued, "is so severe that we are expecting a famine, yet the theatres have been reopened and plays are being produced with the best actors."

A play? An audience ready to attend it? It seemed unbelievable.

The other letter was from a man living in Bavaria. He had been imprisoned for many months on suspicion of having conspired against Hitler, and wrote to tell us that he had survived and had returned home where he found nothing changed. He had just taken a trip to Western Germany by car to attend a business meeting and described the fruit ripening on trees, towns being reconstructed and the peaceful activities of the countryside.

"It is a beginning," Freddy smiled. "Soon life will be as normal here as anywhere."

As the colors were fading at the end of a long hot day, the library door opened and our friend Hedi stood on the threshold. She had travelled from Berlin on foot and by train, taking six hours for barely twelve miles, in such an acute fear of assault on the way that Kerzendorf now seemed to her as remote as Africa. We lived in such isolation that we had given up hope of ever seeing any of our former friends again, and had mentally relegated Hedi to the shadows of the past.

As Freddy and I both secretly feared that we would lose our courage if we admitted to each other the insecurity of our present situation, we never talked about it and faced every new circumstance without comment. We were becoming so unaccustomed to put into words the surprise we constantly felt that our self-imposed silence continued, we would have forgotten how to express it. We had met people who had become petrified from undergoing more than they could stand. No further reactions could be elicited from them. They did not die, yet they were dead. Only the episode which had finally crushed them went on dully revolving in their minds, repeating itself like a cracked gramophone record, while every event that occurred before or after had vanished from their consciousness.

Now we were able to say freely to Hedi what we had not dared tell each other, although we had no intention of complaining against our fate. We had chosen to remain in Kerzendorf for a definite purpose, and it was logical that we should suffer the inevitable consequences of our country's defeat. Yet we were under so great a nervous strain, that only Hedi's genuine concern, forcing us to answer her questions, kept us from falling into the abyss that divided us from insanity. In return we listened to her own experiences, and our mutual sympathy

169

reduced to a human scale the forces that had seemed incalculable.

Yet Hedi brought bad news. The bank where we had stored the most precious part of our collection had become part of the Russian Sector and its contents had been confiscated. Hedi had not managed to remove them in time, for as one set of dangers always succeeded another, street fighting began as soon as the bombs stopped falling. We listened in silence, each of us intent on something we had cared for which was now irretrievably lost.

"But," Hedi went on, "the apartment at the Stein-Platz, lying in the city's district of Charlottenburg, has been included in the British Sector." Again we were silent, speechless at the importance of her words, for they meant not only that we could now return to the capital, but that from now on, whatever happened, we were linked to Europe again.

Hedi told us about life in Berlin, where Quakers were already starting admirable relief work to prevent epidemics brought in by refugees from spreading, an endeavour that at a moment when hatred and hostility were still raging was a moving symbol of humanity. As food was scarce, large scale bartering had begun in improvised markets which kept open day and night, where every conceivable object was exchanged for chocolate and cigarettes. The value of antiques was going up daily, for Russians, who were by far the best clients, spent their lavish pay on porcelain figures and dinner-services at almost any price. The restaurant at the Stein-Platz Hotel close to our flat had reopened, and the proprietor had rented one of the hotel's two undestroyed suites to a hairdresser, and the other to Elizabeth Arden's representative, a German girl who had saved up creams and lotions all through the war and was now giving treatments for as long as her reserves lasted.

These two people had set up shop only one day after the Russians had handed over that part of the town to British occupation. They were overrun with clients from the first moment. Ruins still smoked, streets were encumbered by rubble

170

and infested by thieves, apartments were half demolished, and the most elementary form of order or transport had not been re-established, when women began streaming out of the besieged and looted houses, having spent days and nights shut up in abject terror. In emerging into daylight, the first thing they confronted was a mirror that sharply arrested their attention. While hiding in dark corners or fighting flames, their appearance had meant less to them than if they had been cats or dogs. From that moment onward girls and women sacrificed anything for money to have their hair set and traces of strain removed from their faces. They wanted only to recapture consciousness of themselves and to become lovable once more. To visit the newly-opened shops was their way of expressing the wish to be alive.

Hedi had made the great effort to come to Kerzendorf to spend my husband's birthday with us, for we had always celebrated it gaily. This year we had little to eat, for according to the latest regulations, all the country produce had to be delivered to Berlin, thereby depriving the country in favour of the city, where there was great danger of mass starvation. But Hedi had obtained ingredients for a tiny birthday cake by clever bartering and we brought a bottle of wine out of hiding to make the meal festive. The room was decorated with flowers and a summer wind in the trees threw a quivering green pattern on the library's panelling and books. It was a happy day.

Chapter XV

As THE trains had at last begun to run regularly between Ludwigsfelde and the capital, we decided that the time had come for us to risk the dangers of an expedition to Berlin.

On the afternoon before our departure, Ida and I went to the park to retrieve our buried treasure which we wished to take to Berlin for greater safety. We searched closely and in vain for at least two hours and began to give up hope of ever finding it again. We went on doggedly digging, until finally Ida uttered a cry of delight, for she had struck the box. We quickly took it home, and there slipped what we could of its contents into that best of all hiding-places, the hems of our dresses.

The next day Ida and I started off at dawn to catch the train. We were to be protected on our journey by the company of both Rudolf and Justus Eber, who had found no regular employment and had stayed on in Ludwigsfelde as his daughter's guest. He was intent on repaying her hospitality, and on achieving his other clearly defined aim in life, to eat much, and if possible, to eat well.

"I am prepared to work," he said, "but I am too old; nobody wants my services." So he had chosen the still novel pursuit of exchanging commodities in an endless round, potatoes for shoes, shoes for alcohol, alcohol for fruit, fruit for meat, meat for woollen stockings. It was gloriously satisfying to him as the owner of a few packets of cigarettes or a sack of coal to discover the world and its riches at his feet. For loafers and gamblers it was a revenge upon the successful of yesterday, a triumph over the thrifty and the virtuous, a malicious pleasure to find morality old-fashioned and impotent. In short, Justus Eber had gone into the black market with flying colors and far from being bashful about it, he was electrified with admiration at his own astuteness.

Ida did not restrain her scathing comments. She told him he was a bad old man and held up a mutual acquaintance as an example of more principled behaviour. Eber answered, in a burst of anger, "His wife is sick in bed because she has no soles on her shoes and his children are under-nourished. Who is better in the eyes of God, I who look after my family, or he who refuses to adapt himself to the rules of the day?"

Russian soldiers were patrolling the Ludwigsfelde station. We felt nervous, for watches and other desirable objects knocked gently against my knees as I walked, and Ida was encased in a suit of armour, with a set of twenty-four forks, knives and spoons sewn side by side into the seams of her coat. But before we could be questioned or examined the train pulled in, snorting and puffing.

We quickly scrambled into a freight car that was so full that we could only stand in the compact mass of travellers with our arms glued to our sides, swaying along with them whenever the train swerved around a corner. After twenty minutes we arrived at the boundary of the American Sector of Berlin and caught a glimpse of American uniforms through a corner of the window.

"Thank God," sighed Ida, in an obvious attack on the self-esteem of a young Russian soldier jammed in beside us. He appeared ill at ease in this crowd of hostile people whose looks he understood though he did not know their language.

After several changes of trains and a long walk to find a substitute for a ruined bridge, we stood, for the first time since the end of the war, in the streets of Berlin.

The difference in atmosphere between Kerzendorf and the city took our breath away. Uniforms and the other symbols of defeat were as visible in Berlin as in the country, but here one did not sense the dread of a personal or an impersonal attack that was a continuous element of our daily life at home.

173

Numerous young girls walked about because their places of employment were either bombed or closed, and took advantage of their enforced holiday for a stroll on this bright, late autumn morning. We stared at them incredulously, for they were carefully made up and their hair curled, while in the Russian Zone they would have made as great an effort to look as inconspicuous as possible. I nearly started forward to warn them. Watches were openly displayed on their arms for anyone to rob. In the background men and women with tired, grey faces, wearing ragged clothes, were working in the ruins; all color converged on the happily smiling girls. Their answers to future questions about memories of the end of 1945 would not be: "I was short of food," but "I was eighteen and life lay before me." Older people's faces looked hopelessly exhausted. They were empty of dreams to divert them from the daily struggle.

My first errand was to hire a truck to fetch as many of our possessions from Kerzendorf to the city as it would hold. Once the things my husband cared for most were safe, I hoped to persuade him to escape the tension in the country for a while and come to Berlin for several weeks.

Only drivers living in the Russian Sector could obtain the necessary permits to drive into our Soviet-controlled Zone. They all asked the same question: "Does your village mayor permit you to take furniture away? If not, he might confiscate it and we risk losing our truck." As it would have been a fatal confession of weakness to admit our feeling of insecurity to the local authorities, I was unable to give the assurance, and was regretfully obliged to give up my plan for the time being.

My other reason for coming to the city was to start working for the Red Cross. Hitler had abolished it as being 'international', a word that meant hell and damnation to his narrow mind, and had substituted a party-ridden national organization which was German only and had no connection with the great Swiss-sponsored institution. Since the end of the war the Catholic and Protestant churches were acting as its representatives.

174

There was work to be done for war prisoners, for the repatriation of refugees, for every form of appalling human misery. I was given papers to translate and agreed to go backwards and forwards from Kerzendorf to Berlin twice a week to fetch and deliver them.

"Condense the report about D.Ps.," they told me, "it is too heartrending. People are surfeited with tragedy and cannot bear any more of it. Unless you tone down the truth, the paper will simply not be read."

It was a shock to return to the Stein-Platz after a lapse of so many months to find our block of flats looking like a giant who had come off the worse in a drunken brawl, its roof gone, windows and doors smashed in, the façade grimly bullet-ridden. Before the entrance a high mound of rubble was piled up in an attempt at tidiness. Wearily climbing over the sad funeral pile, I stopped short, for amongst torn bits of wallpaper, rubbish and odds and ends of inert matter I saw an immaculate green plant, its delicate stem waving in the morning breeze, as fresh as if it stood in a fertile field. How could even a small weed have taken root in this derelict litter? Yet here swayed a gracefully impertinent taunt to destruction.

At the back of the house where Hedi and old Pauline lived, the window-panes were intact, but in my room they had been shattered by bullets. Wooden planks let in the cold and shut out all light except for thin rays piercing the gaps like golden needles, so that a candle had to be kept burning all the time. The four walls, cracked by explosions but still erect, had at one time sheltered thirty German soldiers and later withstood the Russian militia storming in and out of its doors.

There were still no telephones, but the news of our arrival got around as if proclaimed by an African tomtom, and in no time neighbours came in to greet us and marvel at our survival and at their own. They were still overcome with surprise at having been caught in situations outside the range of anything they had ever known or imagined, and were possessed of a

175

psychological urge to relive their experiences by describing them to us who had not shared them.

Women were particularly insistent and repetitious in telling exactly when, how and how often they had been raped. Nothing restrained them from dwelling on the painful memory, so that even the most modest did not hesitate to give a prolix description of these insults. They would recite detail upon detail in a matter-of-fact, monotonous tone of voice which was belied by an expression of insanity in their eyes. A characteristic of all these people was that on no account would they listen to the experiences of others, but in their self-absorption hurriedly interrupted them with a still more hair-raising story, until one could but listen in dumb sympathy.

I was anxious to find out who, of all the people I had known, were still amongst the living in Berlin, and I wandered about like Rip Van Winkle in his native town after his many years sleep. The homes of most of our friends were nothing but heaps of stones. No one could tell me if their inhabitants had escaped or died.

I found a friend of my mother's who had just returned from Ravensbruck, one of the concentration camps for women, living in an undamaged apartment that had been preserved for her by a faithful old maidservant.

Her experiences had not embittered her, because she considered the Gestapo, judges and guards as cogs in a clumsy, impersonal machine, and regarded them with a mixture of contempt and dry humour that excluded hatred. Her attitude was in contrast to that of most ex-prisoners, who had become so obsessed by what they had been through, that they related every experience to the time of their captivity, when their wits and nerves had contracted in self-defence. Only those who had shared their identical misfortunes excited their interest; meeting and corresponding with them filled their imagination. Finally a gulf opened between them and their closest friends. The latter became 'those who did not know', while they themselves were martyrs singled out from mankind. Yet they were accepted as such, admiration for them was constant and compassion did not wane, but it became static. Once a saturation point was reached, their unwilling audience would react by an unjust but irresistible inclination to avoid their company.

In 1943 the old lady had been invited to a tea-party by Baroness von Thaden, a prominent member of a Protestant sect, who had asked a former German diplomat to lecture at her house. Another guest was a man who had gained the hostess' confidence by offering to post letters for her or her friends in Switzerland, where he was travelling the following day, without their passing through the German censor; no one had suspected that he was an agent of the Secret Police.

When he arrived, the drawing-room was already full of people. He wandered slowly from group to group, listening to subversive remarks and taking note of allusions to a conspiracy. When the former diplomat, a fanatical opponent of totalitarianism, delivered a speech in which he attacked National-Socialism, the spy jotted it down, and went off with several compromising letters in his pocket. Some days later came the result of his treachery. To set an example, Baroness von Thaden and the lecturer were decapitated for the outspoken expression of their opinions, while the others were sent to concentration camps, among them my mother's friend who was then nearly seventy years old. Now she had the benefit of certain privileges, such as increased food rations and coal supply, for she was an O.D.F., initials that stood for 'Victim of Fascism'.

She told me where to find another old friend of my family, Katinka, Baroness Kardorff, a woman of great ability who had been a prominent member of the Liberal Party and a collaborator of its leader, Stresemann. She and her good-looking, tall, white-haired husband, a moderately right wing politician of great dignity, had taken refuge from the Gestapo and the bombing of the capital in a small village outside Berlin.

At the time, in 1945, when it was incorporated in the Russian Zone, the Russians vehemently advocated a return to democracy in contrast to Fascist slavery, and those who like Katinka and her husband had fought for these ends were officially in high esteem. Katinka came out of her long inaction with zest. In a short time she was elected mayor of the village, which she governed well on Socialist principles; soon order reigned and her popularity was great.

The Communist headquarters of the province regarded her increasing political following with jealous dislike. Yet as the election by which Katinka had been voted mayor was legal, they grudgingly put up with the domination of this efficient and vital lady of seventy.

When late one afternoon three Russians asked to be admitted to the sitting-room of her house to see her on local business, she received them politely, dressed in her long black velvet tea-gown. Two of them immediately pointed loaded pistols at her, while the third man assaulted her. When she gathered herself up, they had vanished. Nothing could be done to identify or punish the soldiers who had been sent to frighten her away from her job. As she had been contaminated by a dreadful disease, she had to go to hospital for many weeks. Now she was cured, but she had to stay in bed, where I found her in the spare room of an acquaintance.

Her husband lay dying, unable to be moved, in the village where she dared not return. Her spirit, however, was not broken. She sat up, burning with indignation, wishing only to fight tyranny under its new guise. She had decided to change over from the Liberal Party to the Social Democrats, and had prepared a speech developing her ideas for school reforms, for orphanages and barracks for D.Ps., which she recited with fiery eloquence interspersed with jokes, gossip and fascinating tales of her life in a spirit of unconquerable youth.

When I got back to the flat it was time to go to bed. For this I was obliged to take off my clothes and dress again as if for a

178

mountain expedition, for the temperature was below freezing-point and the large room was even colder than the street outside. Winds blew in through the planks of the three high windows and through the broken walls. I began by wrapping myself up like a mummy, then wound a turban about my head, imitating the pseudo-Turkish caps with golden tassels worn on retiring by gentlemen in Molière's plays, to keep the draughts at bay. But what about my nose? It stuck out into the icy air unclad and unprotected. One or more pairs of gloves, pulled on one over the other, were of no avail in keeping my hands from becoming numb as they held a book. Hot drops of wax made circles on the pages as they fell, so that I crossly blew out the candle and buried my nose and hands deep under the bedclothes. A rhythmical wave of sleep carried me off and consciousness receded.

I was woken up by a ghostly patter. Where the white moonlight lit up a small portion of the floor, I clearly saw a large circle of mice racing and leaping in the intricate figures of a dance. More coming through cracks in the walls, none had noticed my presence. I was safe if they stayed on the floor, but what if something induced them to jump onto my bed? I watched them for a long time, warily alert while they ran about, their tails swishing, a moonbeam occasionally sparkling in a beady eye. When two of them approached my hanging bedclothes, I whistled in terror. They became motionless; there was absolute silence. After a slight interval, wild whirring started anew, until I interrupted their ballet by another signal and they stopped moving, then danced again and again, until I noticed nothing more.

To restore my circulation, I went to a nearby nursing-home for a hot bath. The waiting-room was heated by a stove and I lingered for a long time in that haven of rest before venturing out into the grim, cold streets of the main thoroughfare, the Kurfurstendamm, where the most outstanding shop-window was Rosen's, a dealer in modern pictures and books. It was a novelty to see on view the works of painters and writers whose names it had been perilous even to mention a few months earlier. I had to re-accustom myself to hear and see the works of such artists as Ney, Trokes, Zimmermann and others who had been obliged to live anonymously for years and were therefore unknown to the public, and hear them discussed freely.

Above Rosen's, up one flight of stairs, was the new hat shop that Madame Marthe had only just opened in place of the one that had been destroyed. As there had been no material for curtains, she had sown white flour sacks together with excellent effect, and in the absence of carpets had painted the floor herself. The premises had been scrubbed to a shiny spotlessness, and she had borrowed mirrors, and procured some green plants, with the tiny sum of money she had taken out of the bank in time. The rest of her possessions had been swallowed up in the universal looting.

She herself was painted and scented as if she had just stepped out of a fashion plate. Nothing on her was casual; hat, dress, scarf, shoes were new and fresh. I asked her politely how she had fared, but her deafness deceived her into thinking that I wanted to confide my troubles to her.

"Don't, dear Madam," she said, "don't look back, let us rather gaze into the future. It is the essence of my particular form of art." Her eyes grew intent. "Could you get hold of a recent number of *Vogue* for me? I would pay any price for it."

The dressmaker next door, Miss Black, was swamped with orders from customers who paid her in food, coffee and cigarettes instead of money. Through a former employee, a pretty Bulgarian model who had married an officer in the Soviet army, she had obtained Russian women as clients, and the evening before had been invited by them to a dinner in a restaurant in their sector. She was fetched by car and taken to a private room where drinking and revelry had already begun. As Miss Black knew no Russian, she could not follow the conversation, and did not feel at ease in the company of people whom she had not ceased to fear.

After much drinking, a violent argument started between the guests, faces reddened, voices grew loud, until a man stood up, knocked over his chair, shouted and shook his fist in fury, while the others drowned his words with cries of anger. When an officer put his hand to his pistol, Miss Black got up terrified, and tried to slip away unnoticed.

The host turned, and seeing her leave, called after her: "Come back and take sides in our quarrel. We are discussing the most important question in the world: 'Is it to a mother or to a father that we owe more affection? Which of the two should we love most?'"

Miss Black reverted to her own problems before we left, and she too clamoured for a copy of *Vogue*. "I absolutely must have it for inspiration," she said. "I promise to make you a coat for nothing if you will get me a copy."

When I entered the Stein-Platz hotel, the dining-room was so crowded that I was made to share a table with the owner of the largest hotel in Berlin, now destroyed, and with the wife of a wine merchant. Both had saved wine and sacks of coffee, which they now tried to barter for coal. Like everybody else, they were frightened at the approach of winter.

I was struck by a group of three men surrounding a tall blonde woman in a new mink coat and a red velvet hat. She was known to have had a romance with one of the Imperial Princes, and though of humble origin herself, only members of the aristocracy found favour in her eyes. Her secret ambition was to marry the handsome bearer of a distinguished name who sat next to her, but the company of intelligent young men had always seemed more attractive to him than that of a vain woman. The persecution by National-Socialism of all he cared for had made him an inveterate enemy of Hitler. The third was a banker who had lost all he owned in Budapest. The four people were in business together, and according to them, worked

181

very hard. That meant that they ran breathlessly in search of profitable business from one shady character to another, in comparison to whom they were mere amateurs. Jewels were their chief commodity, for even the most inferior varieties were eagerly sought after and bought by D.Ps. willing to pay inflated prices for diamonds or precious stones and metals easily transportable from country to country.

They were conversing in whispers about their various speculations in dollars, pounds or Swiss francs, warning each other about certain faked notes. Despite the haze of money surrounding them, they were haunted by the perpetual fear of blackmail, arrest or heavy losses. Prices unaccountably soared or fell, and as they owned no capital, it was certain ruin if the goods they had bought should prove unsellable, so they kept nothing, but passed everything on at once to someone else. All they snatched at great effort from this fleeting tide of wealth was to live passably well. The fair beauty had acquired some now fashionable but soon outmoded clothes, and her friends wore new suits.

I was glad to get away from them. At the end of the train journey and the long walk from the station were my beloved warm and light rooms. Scents and sounds in the quiet of the evening vividly evoked memories of earlier home-comings, and made us forget our danger in the sweetness of their recaptured pleasure.

Chapter XVI

I HAD left Berlin and its scrambling ugliness and discomfort to return to Kerzendorf, where the trees in the park had now grown scarlet and the yellow leaves turned to gold as they slowly glided to the ground. Each, having revealed its existence in a flash of sunlight, was extinguished when it reached the earth and became part of a softly rustling carpet. My eyes followed the now slightly neglected, mellowed lines of paths and alleys, seeking consolation in their harmony from the disturbing rumours about land reform.

The land we owned did not exceed the number of acres permitted in the Russian Zone, but the villagers had obtained permission from the Russians to requisition from us a row of houses that my family had built for workmen. But when soon afterwards the roofs needed repair, and the community was taxed to pay for it, the whole village rose in anger at the idea that they should have to meet expenses that until now had been our responsibility.

An important reason behind the division of the land was the political purpose of breaking up the leadership of the Prussian gentry, whose influence in the Province of Brandenburg had been uncontested for hundreds of years. But there was also the practical need to solve the terrible problem of the refugees, who had to be given a chance to provide for their own living and become normal citizens. There was land enough to satisfy the demands of all, but as the intention of the mayor and his friends was to augment their own possessions under cover of imperfectly formulated orders, they had decided to take all gardens belonging to peasants or to us, and redistribute them according to their fancy.

The Zarns, Monks and others were as desperate as we were at this arbitrary confiscation, but there was no possible defence against it. Since everyone had the right to a certain number of acres, nobody could protest even if waste land was allotted to them in return for fertile soil. The refugees buzzed like mosquitoes, believing that now at last the hour for retribution had come, but as they were convinced that they alone deserved the best land in compensation for their sufferings and exile, the standard of their expectations could not possibly be satisfied. I stayed in my room during this period of oppressive agitation, turning over in my mind plans for next year's planting—if they would let me. I sat in my large chair, too worried to read, trying in vain to lose myself in the contemplation of a cluster of bright berries that glowed in a pewter bowl on a low table beside me.

Freddy had just returned discouraged from a discussion with the Mayor, when a moment later his representative, Fisher, asked to see him. As he bowed and sat down, I felt a repulsion towards his coarse, sly face and shifty eyes that he kept fixed on the hat he was turning in his hands.

"The Russian authorities have received some letters denouncing you as an anti-communist influence," he began, "and they have ordered us to exile you to another district. It is lucky that the Mayor and myself are your friends, for we are free to interpret regulations as we please."

I tried to remain motionless, and not betray my feelings.

"If you are sent away, all you possess becomes village property," he went on. "This is not in our own interests as it might form a precedent that could later be applied to any one of us. So I have come to give you some useful advice. Apply to the Russians for permission to be listed as a 'Klein-Bauer', a small-scale farmer, and we will support your application. If it is accepted, you will no longer be considered as belonging to the obnoxious class of landowners, and your right to live in Kerzendorf cannot be contested." He got up, and turned round as he reached the door: "I forgot to mention that as I must use my position while it lasts to build myself a home, I shall require the bricks of your bombed building and the ground on which they stand."

He sighed and went on. "The Mayor and his wife need the part of the orchard containing the peach-trees, the raspberry bushes and the corn. If you sign a paper relinquishing all of this to us, we will guarantee you in return the house you live in, the park and the remaining part of the kitchen-garden. We also promise not to touch your employees' property."

There was a heavy silence, broken by Fisher's mirthless laugh. "If you refuse, we will not obtain what we want, but then you, of course, are bound to lose everything. You will be permitted to keep a cow," he said now facing us, "and as it happens, I have an excellent one to sell. Do you agree to the bargain?"

Freddy looked at me across the room. I knew that there was no choice but to give in.

We assented. The Mayor appropriated the greater part of the garden I had planted and tended. Fisher took over the ruins of the house, the stables and the garage.

We waited week after week for the Russian commission, that was to confirm what had been but a private agreement. The ground on which we had trodden now seemed to rock; rooms and trees from which we might soon be torn lost all reality.

When Fisher brought the large, placid cow on a long rope, we felt that he would take her away again when it suited him. People's curious stares mocked at our defencelessness in a mixture of pity and greed. Villagers and refugees came every day with rapacious demands for our furniture, bedclothes or cooking utensils. They asked for more far more, than we owned, saying under their breath, "When you are forced to leave, you will be able to take nothing with you," or more menacingly, "We will see to it that the Russians come and fetch it for us."

The growing tension was augmented by an absurd situation I was placed in by Bibi. Of every month in the year, of all moments

185

of our life, thoughtless Providence had chosen these days in which to concentrate attention on us. Bibi was in a condition that made her intensely interesting to the whole canine world of Kerzendorf and its neighbourhood. Big and small, young and old dogs flocked in from every side, glaring and growling at each other in grim jealousy. Day and night they howled, whined and panted, staring unhappily towards the entrance of the house. They made the shortest walk embarrassing by closing in on Bibi and me, yet, if an admirer dared approach her, she nearly bit his nose off. Bibi languorously reclined on a cushion from which she lifted her troubled eyes to mine, and at intervals gave out a short yelp that was answered by a chorus of wailing. "Disgusting behaviour," said Ida; "it should be stopped."

Our anxiety prevented us from sleeping. Our thoughts revolved in a circle of conjectures about the discussions between Russians and Germans that we guessed to be going on behind our backs. At last a commission was announced and a few days later the district commander arrived with the officers who had been detailed to investigate our case. The Mayor and Fisher kept their promise by speaking in our favour. Peasants were questioned, and testified that I had for months worked the soil as conscientiously as themselves. The Russian officials agreed to the German suggestion that we should be recognized as Kerzendorf farmers, and approved of the idea that we should take over some of a neighbour's hens. They then visited the cow, which to my distress had developed a cough. The officers, who had been peasants themselves in their pre-war lives, were full of sympathy for her and went over her small stable with me in a genuine desire to be helpful, until they discovered a hole in the wall letting in the cold draught that had affected her health. Before leaving, they helped me to fill it up with chalk and straw.

The weeks of heavy strain that had taken from autumn until February of 1946 had ended happily. Not only were we to be allowed to remain in Kerzendorf, but we now had sufficient eggs and milk, and need no longer fear malnutrition. "Logic and justice always win," said Freddy when the men had gone, but it took time for us to recover our nervous balance, and we emerged from this period as if from a long illness. My husband had to see his lawyer, and I was obliged to go to the Red Cross. "Everything is safe here now," we remarked to each other, looking at the courtyard and garden that formed a picture of peace.

We both tacitly hoped to get away for a day or two, even if it meant struggling for food and fighting off the cold in Berlin. The long walk to the station on a day much below freezing-point was tiring for Freddy's heart, but we went along gaily. When we had secured seats in the train, a sense of escape overcame me, and to hide it I buried my eyes in a book.

I started up on hearing someone call out our name. To my consternation the conductor was trumpeting it out again, and told us to go home at once.

The next moment we were anxiously hastening back along the same slippery road that we had only just covered in peace of mind. At home the quiet scene we had left but an hour before was now seething with soldiers. They were to be billeted in our house and around the farmyard, and the stables were cleared for horses. We had stacked cases of china and various other collections, such as mathematical instruments, old thimbles and snuffboxes, in a shed so small that no horse could possibly have been stabled in it. Just as we arrived a group of refugees were urging the soldiers to break open the door thinking that they would find behind it unheard-of treasures. When Freddy opened it with a key there was a rush forward. Boxes were torn open in a fever of cupidity, their contents scattered on the floor, and in a second many hands were holding, appraising and grabbing at what they could.

When everything made of metal had vanished the soldiers roughly ordered the rest to be thrown out into the courtyard.

For a long time I searched in the mud and straw to retrieve some objects, mixed up with old letters, photographs of lovely, smiling women and girls in ball dresses whose cardboard faces had been trodden on and bent. When all was quiet again the farmer's wife from next door arrived and let me store what was left in her loft.

The six soldiers who had been assigned to us took a room at the top of the house. They were modest in their demands and thanked me for everything I did to make them comfortable. "We don't need washstands," they protested, "we will use the pump in the courtyard."

One of them was a tall blond Esthonian called Peter. "My father had a large estate," he told me. "It was confiscated and he was sent to Siberia. You can rely on me to help you whenever I can."

A dull sound made me look towards the window. Two or three hundred horses were galloping through the gate, followed by soldiers hoarsely shouting and cracking whips. I flew downstairs, out of the house, while laughing and cursing riders pressed the surging mass of fine strong beasts through shrubs and bushes. The horses reared, stood quivering on their hind legs and then plunged forward. Small trees were violently bent, and fragile statues made of sandstone were upset and broken, while the soldiers played ball with their heads and excited the animals to a frenzy, until they were covered in white foam and the lawn was deeply marked by the brown imprint of their hooves.

From then on, we lived in the midst of a herd of horses, whose neighing woke us in the morning when the stables were opened to let them loose in the park. We were surrounded by a chorus of gruff voices from the soldiers living in the room above mine. When women visited them in the evening, I was an unwilling audience to their singing, revelry and quarrels ending in shrill screams for help. Once a man was thrown down the stairs against my door with such violence that it cracked and split.

188

Every two hours when the guards for the horses were changed, heavy boots clumped down the steps to the accompaniment of singing.

Freddy tried to pacify my fears and Bibi's indignation by saying, "It is normal soldiers' behaviour. You are wrong to mind it."

In February, on the day of the carnival, a fancy-dress ball took place in Kerzendorf that finished up in the room above mine. People came and went, knocked at my door and shouted while I sat on my bed all night long with my coat on. At dawn three drunken men stood outside beating their fists and kicking heavily against the flimsy wood in their efforts to get in. Through the noise I heard Peter urging them upstairs, and he whispered through the keyhole: "Sleep, I will keep them off." After he had hustled them away, I heard him squat down on the floor in front of the door, lean against it and then snore, while the stamping and laughter continued. Peter woke from time to time and growled heavily at a new attempt at intrusion. At last daylight brought an end to the siege.

On Ash Wednesday we were the centre of a market. Women stood outside the house waiting the whole day to speak and sell things to the soldiers. I stayed indoors to avoid the crowd, and looked out on to the shifting scene, lit for a few minutes by a pale sun that was soon obscured by erratic falls of snow. I had received copies of the two American and French newspapers, the *Tagesspiegel*, and the *Kurier* and was reading them beside the crackling fire, when there was an alarming knock at the door. I immediately threw them into the flames, for the Russian press alone was allowed in the Russian Zone and other papers were severely forbidden. It was only Ida, but as it was too late to retrieve them, I went on with the two volumes of Jean Paul Sartre's novel.

Many books are just delightful window-displays of jewels and toys and some are voices from space answering questions one has tried in vain to solve. Sartre's novel had the effect on me of

189

a private letter from a contemporary, describing his reactions at a time when war and peace hung in the balance. But the pessimism it eloquently expressed was a message of yesterday, a reflection of the epoch before 1939, when we had suffered the agony of living in a world on the eve of final collapse, when human relationships were menaced by differences of opinion and cruel separations.

Yet in 1946, after the worse predictions had materialized, new catastrophes might occur, but they could not add to our already over-full experience. The survivors discovered to their surprise not only that infinitely more had been left standing than they had been led to expect, but that in fact everything essential was indestructible. The constant possibility of dying had awoken in them a conscious sense of life that was independent of circumstances, and with it detachment from much of the social structure that had been of importance in the pre-war period. For the strong there was the intoxication of existing, the throbbing of arteries, the experience of love even in the pathos of its absence; while for the tired, there was extinction, the lure of death's always open arms.

Freddy lay down, for he was not well, while I went on reading, silently arguing with the author, when about eleven o'clock there was a loud rapping on all the doors, accompanied by threats: "Open, or we shoot our way in." Soldiers entered, pistols in hand. "We want chairs, linen, tables," they said.

"But why do you come for them in the middle of the night?" Freddy asked.

They spoke to each other in Russian; then one of them roared at me: "How can you insult us by being scared? A German soldier lived with my family for two years and was treated like a brother."

It had not occurred to him that their forced entrance did not inspire confidence. They took what they found; then, after whispering together, insisted on my accompanying them to the Mayor, who lived half an hour's walk away. No protest was of any use, although they finally allowed Rudolf to come with me.

They placed us in the middle of their little group so that we should not escape, and walked us through the sleeping village in the bitter cold. They woke up the Mayor, and roughly ordered him to write out slips of paper that were to give legality to the requisition. When we were once again outside in the dark, the soldiers tried to drag me into their cart and drive me to the next village where they were stationed.

Rudolf got between me and the man who was grasping my arm and pushed me through a little door in the wall surrounding a churchyard on the other side of the street. I threw myself flat on the ground behind a tombstone, Rudolf did the same a few feet away from me. From where I lay motionless, I dimly recognized my old nurse's grave in the distance and thought with longing of her unquestioning affection and protection. At last the men gave up searching for us, the cart clattered off and we were saved.

At three in the morning there was more knocking on the door. It was a vet, with his two assistants, who demanded a mirror, an easy chair and a clock. Towards morning several others came to search our cupboards and take away clothes. As soon as I saw Peter I asked him why these visits took place after dark.

"They are forbidden to requisition outside of their own village," he answered. "If you were a peasant you would have the right to complain." "We are peasants, we have been recognized as village farmers," I said angrily, but Peter only shrugged his shoulders. Yet although the Mayor tried to stop the nightly visits that alarmed him as much as ourselves, they continued, probably stimulated by people hostile to ourselves, who put the soldiers up to it.

After my husband had recovered, it was my turn to be ill, as a result of my forced outing, and it was from my bed I heard some officers ask to speak to Freddy. When four men had

191

entered and sat down on the sofa in the library, one of them said in an aggressive tone:

"We have information that you were once a diplomat, and we want details of your career, where you were posted, and how much you were paid." I wished I could have gone in to reply in Freddy's place, or been able to interrupt him before he said too much. Instead of that I had to listen to him answering the whole truth, that seemed harmless to him, while the mere mention of cities like Paris, Washington or Lisbon sounded sinister to indoctrinated minds. In my anxiety I began to pray that God would inspire Freddy to give soothing answers when they wished to know what he thought of conditions in the Russian Zone, and asked him if he had read Stalin's works. Then the voices reverted to the weather and finally they took their leave.

Freddy entered my room with a pale face. After an interval of brooding he looked at me. "I ought to die," he said. "Then you could leave."

"Let us leave together," I said.

"I have committed myself, I cannot change my mind."

"You must live. Promise to live. I do not understand life, nor people, nor money. I shall be lost."

"My imagination is dead. I can no longer adapt myself, but you can." Then in a change of mood: "After all, it was their duty to question me. Besides, they were very polite."

Chapter XVII

THE NEXT day, which was March 1, 1946, we left for Berlin without further incident. The train stopped for a moment at the first station in the American Sector. The headlines of a *Kurier* caught my eye : "Abolition of Zonal Frontiers by the end of the year." I reached out of the window and bought the paper, to find an article based on an interview with General Clay, couched in vaguer terms than the heading. "You see," Freddy insisted; and then, "Look at this," pointing to the words: "Postal communication with abroad will be permitted from April onwards." "In the long run there is but one climate in Europe," he concluded. "We who live only a few miles from the capital are part of it."

Having done various errands, we lunched with Charles, who had left his parents' house in the Russian Zone to live and work in Berlin. We sat quietly talking, surrounded by drawings, bronzes and books, and looked out on the undramatic tops of pine trees. Each of us lived where the explosion of defeat had projected him, and was governed by needs so contrasting that it meant an effort to understand the laws and motives of the others' behaviour.

Charles was still living in the sheltered nineteenth-century way of life of money, stability and plans for the future. All these had been thrown overboard, and we had returned to the beginning of the Middle Ages, to the period of the great migrations. The breath of dark hordes was hot on our necks, driving us on, blowing out of our hands all we were desperately trying to hold. We saw his tidy world lying behind a glass pane and longed for its security, well realizing that under the sway of barbarism we ourselves had been turned into barbarians. We refrained with difficulty from using expressions that would bring an unsuitably tragic tone to the peaceful atmosphere of his room. We had to use all our tact to remain on common ground and avoid imperilling our friendship.

I walked leisurely to the Stein-Platz and had just put out my hand to ring the bell of the front door, when I was confronted by a strange man who accosted me in a rolling foreign accent. He was heavy and uncouth looking, about fifty, wore no uniform, and on this warm, wet day wore a huge fur cap on his head.

He was waiting for my husband, he declared, and started questioning me. "When is he expected back? What is he working at?" It was imperative that he should see him, and he tried to follow me into the house. I stood in the rain, refusing to let him in, begging him to tell me who had sent him, and to tell me, instead of Freddy, what he had come to say.

"It is nothing unpleasant," he kept repeating, in a way that failed to reassure me. I pressed him to reveal his nationality. "I am not a Russian," he said, but was he telling the truth?

"I shall be back in front of the house tomorrow at this hour with further instructions," was all I could obtain. I went in to Hedi and found her alarm as great as mine, for the same man had come two or three times lately to look for Freddy in a mysteriously inquisitive manner.

When my husband arrived we begged him to leave for Kerzendorf at once, for it looked too much like a plan to kidnap him, to risk staying in Berlin. For a moment he hesitated, then decided against leaving before the next day. He was looking forward to spending an evening at the new night-spot, the 'Royal Club', and to dancing, which he loved. "I need it," he said, and laughed. "I must have some fun for once," and would not be persuaded.

I had planned to go and listen to a quartet that had been playing regularly for some weeks. Its most prominent artist was a
gifted cellist who had not appeared in public since 1933. As his
attractive and musical wife was Jewish, he would have been
forced to divorce her after 1933 to go on giving concerts, so he
had lived in retirement, on very little money, working and
developing his art in solitude for twelve long years, in the continual hope of resuming his career after this interminable period
of frustration.

When we arrived at the theatre where the performance was
to take place, we were turned away at the entrance and told
that in the afternoon a motor accident had put an end to the
cellist's life. He had treated the last years merely as a transitory
interruption to his freedom, and now fulfilment had eluded
him. His friends were bitter at the unbearable irony of fate, yet
his life, as we looked back on it, did not seem to us, as it did
to them, an unfinished sketch, but a perfectly composed and
completed picture, the portrait of a man who had sacrificed his
aspirations to a human attachment and to his integrity. It had
not brought him material satisfaction, but his unexpected end,
with its lack of recompense, shone with stronger light than a
long period of success.

The next morning Hedi came to see me with her face streaming with tears as a result of a conversation she had had with my
husband. "I promised not to tell you, so as not to worry you,"
she went on repeating, until at last she consented to explain. A
young couple of well-known anti-fascists, who until now had
lived fairly undisturbed in their country house in the Russian
Zone, had been at the Royal Club the night before. In an
interval of the music, Helen, the wife, had crossed the floor and
come up to Freddy. "Don't go back to Kerzendorf," she
implored him. "We have heard of an impending move against
all former landowners, and we have decided never to return
home again."

"My heart, my books, my clothes, warmth and food are there

and nowhere else," Freddy answered, shaken but stubborn. "Do not spoil this evening's charm, a lovely woman should not utter ugly warnings. Let us dance," and he had stayed late. Yet to Hedi he admitted how moved he was. "My friends wanted me to remain in Berlin and my wife asks me to escape to the country," he added. "One cannot spend one's time in running away."

Freddy was shaving when I went to speak to him, and at first would not answer at all. We could decide nothing before we knew what the afternoon's interview with the stranger would bring. If it went well, we would return to Berlin at the end of April for a week or two. To prepare for this, Hedi promised to find someone who would fill up the worst cracks in the walls of our rooms, and try to get some window-panes to replace the rough wooden planks that shut out the daylight and let in the cold.

Shortly before two o'clock, I was pacing the street outside the house. A few minutes later the sinister individual appeared. His expression had become less forbidding. "I am authorized to put you in touch by telephone with my chief," he announced. "Come to the post-office with me, and I'll get him for you." I followed him distrustfully, and watched him dial. He handed me the receiver, and to my astonishment I found an American officer at the other end.

Friends in America had asked an acquaintance to find out if we had survived the war, and not knowing if we spoke English, he had used a Lithuanian as an interpreter to make inquiries. I rushed back to give Hedi and Freddy the good news.

Freddy was irritated. "You all live in a childish world of murder stories," he said. "Let us take the next train for Kerzendorf."

As I went down the passage to get my coat, old Pauline came out of her room and took hold of my arm. "I must speak to you," she urged. I stood still to listen, in a hurry to go. "Don't

196

leave for Kerzendorf," her hand gripped me. "Last night your mother appeared to me in a dream. She cried out in an agony of distress and ordered me to warn you that something terrible would happen to you if you went home."

I heard Freddy's voice: "Come on, we will miss the train." I was impatient. "You are wrong to frighten me in this way, Pauline, just as we're leaving."

"She told me to warn you. She warns you," Pauline desperately called after me as the front door shut behind us with a click.

"You must not be upset by an old woman's superstition," said Freddy, attempting to calm me. What could she mean? What could my mother mean? I thought of train accidents, of wayside robberies.

"I am tired," I heard Freddy say, "I wish we were home already." We were both tired, but he was totally exhausted. The train journey was interrupted by interminable walks where explosions had blown up tracks and bridges. We trudged through the heavy mud feeling small as ants in the bleak plain where scraggy trees stood out black against an unending grey horizon. Spring, it seemed, would never grace this sullen land again.

"Next year the bridges will be rebuilt and we shall be able to drive all the way," Freddy said when we had reached the little local train.

As I clambered out of the overflowing compartment onto the Ludwigsfelde platform, a few steps away from me I saw a Russian officer in a trench-coat fixing his eyes on mine, standing rigidly to attention as if the aim of his life was to stare at me and then at my husband. It made me want to hide my face in my hands. I took hold of Freddy's sleeve and pulled him into the midst of the jostling crowd.

As we approached the station barrier, Rudolf came towards us from the other side and I noticed with surprise how pale and drawn his face was.

"Two officers have been waiting to speak to you since this morning," he reported. "They arrived with an interpreter and a car." Behind him stood a tall dark man in a grey tweed coat, with a large Oriental nose, a big mouth and a half mocking, half obsequious manner.

"My name is Androff," he introduced himself. "These two gentlemen," he indicated the officers, one of whom was the one I had noticed, "wish me to interpret some questions to you. We can take you home in our car."

Freddy was by now feeling so unwell that his first reaction was gratitude at being spared an hour's walk. He leaned back with his eyes shut, while the officers sat inscrutably looking out on to the wintry fields, and the interpreter kept up a rattling conventional conversation that I tried to answer politely.

When we arrived home, one of the officers stayed in the car, while the two other men entered the house with us. The civilian started the interrogation. "I am sorry to bother you," he began, "but I am simply carrying out my orders. Until when did you work for the Foreign Office?"

"Till 1933," my husband answered.

"Then you need fear nothing," Androff said. "Do you possess any official papers?" They went next door, where Freddy dug out the only copy of an old diplomatic report he happened to have kept. While the interpreter looked through his personal papers, to my embarrassment I was left alone in the library with an enormously tall officer standing erect with one hand on his pistol. He looked down at Bibi whom I was holding tight to stop her from barking and to give me confidence by feeling her warm little presence. Sensing my nervousness, she started trembling.

"Is the dog frightened?" the officer asked in faltering German, and, seeing me speechless, added, looking past me with a childlike, serious expression: "I am not a bad man."

Freddy and Androff came in again, the interpreter filling the room with his chatter. He demanded to look through my desk.

He sat down in front of it, opened the drawers and snatched out letters at random, perused one from a woman just back from a concentration camp, tossed indifferently aside a letter which was written in French.

"What is this?" he said suspiciously, taking up my photographs of paintings.

"I am interested in painting," I explained.

"So am I," he replied, and took up a postcard representing a school for cats, that I had bought to send to a child. He looked at it in fascination, and asked if he might keep it.

He then addressed himself to Freddy. "We accuse you of nothing, but we want you to accompany us to the headquarters of the NKVD, the secret police, so that we can take down what you said in a protocol, and ask you a few questions about the working of the Foreign Office. It is now Saturday, six o'clock; you will probably be back tomorrow at the same time, Tuesday at the latest."

We were stunned for a moment; then I started forward, asking if I could come along with them. "Impossible," the interpreter smiled. My heart raced. Would Freddy answer satisfactorily? Could he stand the excitement? What sort of accommodation would they give him?

"Don't worry, your husband has nothing to fear," Androff continued. "He will have a heated room. Give him a blanket for the night, but quickly, we must leave."

I rapidly got a rug, bread, soap. "A book," Freddy asked, "Tolstoy's *War and Peace*."

For a second I managed to speak to him alone. "Whom shall I ask for help? What shall I do?"

From next door Androff was urging us to be quick. Freddy was nearly fainting. He stood for a moment, jingling the keys in his pocket. "Go and see Charles on Monday morning," he whispered.

There was a feeling of sharp tension, putting the soldier on his guard, as though he were expecting an attack from one of us. I took first the soldier, then the interpreter, by their hands and begged them to be kind to Freddy, repeating myself in the bustle and scraping of feet that drowned my words.

There was a banging of doors. A cold wind blew in. I felt Freddy kiss me.

I never saw him again.

Chapter XVIII

RECENTLY, WHEN the immediate peril seemed to have passed, it had been possible to take off one's armour and resume the business of being alive. Now, awake or asleep, moving or resting, the world was filled with anxiety and contained nothing else. At first, I stood in the sudden stillness of our room with Androff's reassuring words ringing in my ears. There was an unacknowledged dread at the back of my mind. Why should the Secret Police wish to keep Freddy for longer than two days? As I paced the room, the singing and commotion starting upstairs seemed but a slight disturbance compared with Freddy's absence. Overwhelming self-reproach made me stand motionless for a moment. I was not sure if my husband had remembered to take the medicine necessary for his heart, and I was certain that he had left his toothbrush behind.

At eight o'clock on Sunday I was woken up by Ida bursting into my room. "Ten or twelve officers have come and are searching through everything. I refused to let them in before you are dressed."

When I was ready, Ida left the door. It swung open to let in a group of men. All but two of them were in uniform, Androff and another interpreter, a young and chubby man, who belied his kindly aspect by great grimness of manner. I was struck by seeing Freddy's bunch of keys, strung on a ring I had given him, dance in the fingers of this stranger. Where, during what scene, could they have been taken from my husband?

The man snarled at me, asking what safes, what secret vaults the keys fitted. "Where are the bars of gold, the diamonds, the treasures?" the interpreter specified. One of the keys fitted Freddy's desk, others belonged to suit-cases or to furniture destroyed in the bombed house, some, to their incredulous irritation, I did not recognize. They wished me to lead them to the ruins, to show them the places where the keys had been used. Of the two officers who escorted me, one was a fat squat man with small, suspicious eyes, who talked threateningly to me between his teeth, while the other assented by fiercely nodding his head. He looked like a hawk, with a lean dark face, and wore a black Astrakan cap at a rakish angle. He was shod in elegant boots made of white felt and black leather.

As they found nothing to satisfy them, they angrily walked me back and started looking for papers. Androff took two porcelain parrots standing on my desk and put them in his pocket. The others gathered up all the small objects they found lying around. Meanwhile the cherub continued his aggressive questioning about perfectly innocuous letters, then ordered me to show them the way to the cellar.

"Please put your coat on, you might catch cold," said Androff with solicitude, reminding me to keep warm while watching myself being robbed.

Downstairs they broke our trunks open and tore out the clothes. They had a special interest in evening gowns of tulle or chiffon, examining them carefully before making a bundle of them. The hawk gallantly offered me a cigarette.

I was led back upstairs, and the searching and questioning went on for four or five hours, until they decided to leave. They removed rugs, curtains, china and cushions, and ripped the leather off the chairs, before throwing everything into a large truck that they had brought with them. They slipped and tripped each other up, bowed down under the weight of what they carried.

I followed them outside, and interrupted them by the repeated question: "When will my husband return?" but they were too absorbed to listen. The young interpreter looked at me with an impersonal, frigid stare that made his face old and cruel, and said in a flat tone, "We will repeat our visit soon."

After they had gone, I found the other inmates of the house

in a state of terror. As I hastened to see the Mayor, Peter brushed past me. "There is nothing to be done when the Secret Police are involved. Leave here at once," he rapidly murmured.

The Mayor telephoned a complaint to the district commander. "We can do nothing with the Secret Police."

The Gestapo, I knew, had also been in the habit of stealing after making an arrest. But was Freddy under arrest? I tried to face the fact, but could not, would not. I returned to the house to still the mounting wave of panic within me by remaining there quietly for the rest of the day.

On Monday morning early when I went to Berlin, everybody I spoke to was convinced that my husband would be back in a day or two and told me not to worry. I went back to Kerzendorf, and there waited for him to return at any minute, but only the same set of men reappeared, and took away whatever they fancied. It was particularly trying to stand by while curtains were pulled down with a jerk by a man who then nonchalantly slung them over his shoulder, or to be insulted for protesting against being forced to get up from a chair so that it could be carried out of the room. It was unpleasant, it was humiliating, but it scarcely seemed to matter when I was constantly on the alert for the bell to ring. When it did, it was never Freddy who stood at the door.

When I asked people in Berlin for help, I found sympathy, but also a curious impotence. The prayers I uttered stopped in mid-air and fell to the ground lifeless, for somewhere between Freddy and me, between me and those under whose power he stood, was a high wall of cotton-wool. No sign, no sound, no communication could penetrate it.

I went to see a venerable statesman who was supposed to have influence with the Russians. While I told my story, I saw his head slowly fall forward in sleep, for he was old and exhausted by a long day. Desperately I spoke louder to revive him, until he opened his eyes wide with a great effort and looking through me said, "Patience, my child, have patience."

There was a business man, said to have the best connections with those who were sure to set Freddy free at once. But when I met him by appointment at a bar, he was very drunk, and proved to be nothing but a gangster. I had to escape from him precipitately.

There was the brisk man who said sharply, "Give it up. It is hopeless." But he failed to convince me.

I was brought into contact with a lawyer who asserted he could buy the release of prisoners. I paid and paid all and more than I had, and was taken in by a crook.

Other women who were in the same predicament as myself had gone through similar experiences, and none of the many I consulted had achieved any more than I had. One was the wife of a scholarly museum director, whose name, by ill-luck, was the same as that of an unrelated SS officer, and he had therefore been arrested and disappeared by mistake. The wife of a French prisoner was being searched for in vain by the French. Another's husband had been taken off because he had played a part in the conspiracy against Hitler, for it was a sign of dangerous independence to have been a rebel. Russians automatically suspected a man who was neither a fascist nor a communist of being anti-totalitarian on principle. Party officials and high party members were released after a short captivity, while intellectuals or anyone connected with the Anglo-Saxon world were imprisoned indefinitely.

In Kerzendorf looting soldiers followed in the wake of the police to take whatever they wanted. I used to sleep in Berlin and went out to Kerzendorf in the early mornings. On the way from the station I trembled at every shadow, but as soon as I had entered the garden my happiness at being where I belonged caused every feeling of fear to vanish.

One day I was persuaded to go back to Kerzendorf no more. There was no leave-taking, no final goodbye, the curtains went down unexpectedly. On a sunny May afternoon as I walked as usual along the garden-paths which were as familiar to me as my own hands, I had no premonition that it was for the last time, and realized only much later that I had been swept away from home for ever. On paper everything continued to belong to me, my ownership was not contested, but I could no longer be there to defend it.

In my absence from Kerzendorf I set out to make the little apartment at the Stein-Platz habitable. It was a test of vitality, and a thrilling contest with adverse circumstances, to succeed gradually in getting the walls repaired, or to obtain window-glass and a stove in negotiations worthy of the foundation of an Empire. The reward for my efforts was that I began to take root again, but the transplantation was irksome, for when summer came I chafed against the absurdity of my forced separation from Kerzendorf. Now that trains ran normally again, the trip only took half an hour, but the Russian Zone was at a distance that could not be measured in terms of time. On Sunday afternoons in June and July I was sick with longing for the roses and scent of jasmine, and staring at the blue sky through the gaps of the ruins opposite, I felt imprisoned until evening. Dusk brought relief, for then friends returned from their excursions, and windows that had been closed against the heat were opened to the cool night and the stars. Later, the sound of steps on the pavement and the laughter of people strolling past were woven into the tapestry of sleep.

One day I went off to the mountains for a rest and to be at liberty in the open air. When I returned to Berlin, where my life now was, a friend met me at the station and gave me the first news of my husband. It had come through a prisoner released from a camp where they had both been held captive.

It was then August 1948. I was told that Freddy had died of starvation a year and a half before, and that he was buried at the edge of the camp with many of his companions. Others had survived, a few had been released for no apparent reason, many of them were still, and are now, in captivity. My husband,

205

like all the others, had never been questioned or tried. He had never been given any opportunity to defend himself.

A number of meagre details gave me a glimpse of an unknown world of people totally abandoned to want and the brutality of their guards. Although the prisoners' physical condition became daily worse, not one of them doubted of his own speedy liberation, and the days passed quickly with the formation of projects for the future, and plans for mutual help once they were set free. I was told of a man whom the Russians had caught like a hare because they needed him as a camp doctor, and he had become too useful for them ever to release him. Under pressure of endless captivity he had given up all concern for himself, and lived solely for the care and consolation of his fellow prisoners.

These terrible camps are one of the most significant phenomena of our times. The monstrous asceticism they have imposed, and are imposing, on millions is crushing not only the lives but the personalities of human beings.

Yet one hears of men and women who have found perfect happiness in a selfless devotion to people around them lost in hopeless despair. Our irreligious, outwardly materialistic age is producing the saints in whose existence we had ceased to believe. Although they are completely cut off from the rest of the world, their names and actions are carried over the highest prison walls like sparks by the wind, and possibly it is they who will be considered greater contemporaries than our generals or scientists. They obey an ideal of humanity reawakened in them, as in us, in contrast or as a compensation to mass indifference, so that we may feel that as well as standing at the end of an epoch, we are also witnessing a renaissance of moral behaviour. In an era of stress it is this spiritual effort that can be our century's expression of art and later become the material from which art takes its source.

The fact stood out with startling cruelty that although my husband had been imprisoned at only an hour's distance by car from the Stein-Platz where I was living, I had been unable to get a word or a piece of bread across this short distance. We had been defeated along the whole line; we had lost against impersonally hostile forces. Yet though before his death Freddy had already suffered more than losing a life that he had always been willing to risk, I was convinced that even in captivity he could not have imagined it possible to have fled before putting up a fight. Memories of the solemn ceremonies usually accompanying death—a religious service, mourning, words and letters expressing sympathy—and the thought of visiting a grave to cover it with flowers, went through my mind. But innumerable women of our time have no right to an outward manifestation of grief; the death of those they loved is washed over by silence.

I had now no further reason for remaining in Berlin, all the less so since the blockade had restricted and changed the city's existence. My departure was decided upon, time hurled me forward towards the hour, the minute, when I had to leave all that surrounded and protected my existence until then. When the car arrived and I reluctantly drove off to get the plane, I found the airfield enveloped by an impenetrable white fog. Flying on that day was out of the question.

I returned to the Stein-Platz, hardly able to believe that a wish I would not have dared to formulate could have been so miraculously granted. Bibi greeted me with a delight mixed with reproach, as if I had gone for a walk without taking her along, and Ida was patient and subdued on that day as she had never been before. I was a ghost allowed back for a short twenty-four hours' reprieve, of which every second contained an element of conscious happiness, even though time was slipping away mercilessly and final separation was inevitable.

Again, as on the day before, I took leave of Ida, stroking Bibi in her arms for the last time, said goodbye to tiny sobbing old Pauline and shook Rudolf's hand.

Then I found myself on the road where many others had preceded me.